# THE COLLECTED WORKS
# OF HERMAN DOOYEWEERD

*Series B, Volume 22*

GENERAL EDITOR: D.F.M. Strauss

# Political Philosophy

*Select Essays*

*Series B, Volume 22*

Herman Dooyeweerd

PAIDEIA PRESS

**Library of Congress Cataloging-in-Publication Data**

Dooyeweerd, H. (Herman), 1894-1977.
   [Lecture Series in the US. English 1960 / Edited 1999]
   Political Philosophy – Slected Essays / Herman Dooyeweerd
   p. cm

   Includes bibliographical references, glossary, and index
   ISBN 978-0-88815-221-3

1. Philosophy. 2. Christian Philosophy. 3. Historicism.
Title.

This is Series B in the continuing series The Collected
Works of Herman Dooyeweerd
(Initially published by *Mellen Press*, now published
by *Paideia Press*)

ISBN 978-0-88815-334-0

The Collected Works comprise a *Series A,* a *Series B,* and a *Series C*

(*Series A* contains multi-volume works by Dooyeweerd,
*Series B* contains smaller works and collections of essays,
*Series C* contains reflections on Dooyeweerd's philosophy
designated as: *Dooyeweerd's Living Legacy*, and
*Series D* contains thematic selections from Series A and B)

A CIP catalog record for this book is available from the British Library.

The Dooyeweerd Centre for Christian Philosophy
Redeemer College Ancaster, Ontario
CANADA L9K 1J4

All rights reserved. For information contact

©PAIDEIA PRESS 2012, Reprinted 2023
Jordan Station, ON., L0R 1S0
www.paideiapress.ca

Printed in the United States of America

# Foreword

The Agreement between The Edwin Mellen Press and The Dooyeweerd Centre (October 16, 1996) states in article 11 that "these vol-umes will not duplicate, in toto, the content of the hardcover volumes and that they may contain contributions by other editors or authors to supplement what is in the Collected Works."

The present Volume contains selections from three different Volumes of the Collected Works of Dooyeweerd published by The Edwin Mellen Press (Lewiston, N.Y.):

(i) Essays in Legal, Social, and Political Philosophy – Series B, Volume 2 (1998) of the Collected Works of Herman Dooyeweerd: The Christian Idea of the State (pp.121-155); The relation of the individual and community from a legal philosophical perspective (pp.91-98).
(ii) A New Critique of Theoretical Thought – Series A, Volume 3 (1997) of the Collected Works of Herman Dooyeweerd: The Structural Principle of the State (pp.411-451).
(iii) Roots of Western Culture, Pagan, Secular, and Christian Options – Series B, Volume 3 (1999) of the Collected Works of Herman Dooyeweerd: Classical Humanism (156-170).

The Introductory Essay by David Koyzis (Redeemer College, Ancaster, Ontario, Canada) provides a well-documented orientation to Dooyeweerd's political philosophy.

I am convinced that this Volume will help many students to read first-hand some of the most challenging and illuminating analyses of Dooyeweerd on issues in the field of political philosophy – particularly in the contemporary intellectual climate where change is emphasized at the cost of constancy and where an understanding of constant structural principles underlying various positive forms of societal institutions is challenged.

*Daniël, F.M. Strauss*
(General Editor)

# Contents

**Foreword**

**Introductory Essay**
**Political theory in the Calvinist tradition   1**
*Dooyeweerd's unique contribution* . . . . . . . . . . . . . . . . . . . . . 5
*Politics and the state* . . . . . . . . . . . . . . . . . . . . . . . . . . . . . . . 7
*Power and justice: transcending another false polarity* . . . . . . . . . . . 11

### The Christian Idea of The State

Emil Brunner rejects the Christian idea of the state . . . . . . . . . . . . . . . 17
National-Socialism and Fascism and the idea of the Christian state . . . . . . . . 18
The ever new, inspiring idea of the Christian state and the
causes of its decline . . . . . . . . . . . . . . . . . . . . . . . . . . . . . . . . . 18
Synthesis and Antithesis . . . . . . . . . . . . . . . . . . . . . . . . . . . . . . 18
Actually, there is but one radical and Scriptural idea of the Christian state . . . 19
The contrast of "nature" and "grace" is non-Scriptural.
Scripture posits the heart as the religious center of human existence . . . . . . 19
The pagan view that "reason" is the supra-temporal center
of a person's being. . . . . . . . . . . . . . . . . . . . . . . . . . . . . . . . . 20
The effects of compromise of Christian and pagan views.
The scheme of "nature" and "grace" as a result of this compromise . . . . . . 20
Thomas Aquinas on human nature. "Nature" as portal of "grace" . . . . . . . . 20
Aristotle: the pagan idea of the state. The state as the highest
bond of human society, of which all other societal relationships
are but dependent parts . . . . . . . . . . . . . . . . . . . . . . . . . . . . . . 21
The pagan totalitarian idea of the state and its revival in
National-Socialism and Fascism. . . . . . . . . . . . . . . . . . . . . . . . . . 22
The truly Christian view of the state takes its stance in the supra-temporal
root-community of redeemed humanity in Christ Jesus . . . . . . . . . . . . . 22
All temporal societal relationships ought to be manifestations
of the supra-temporal, invisible church of Christ . . . . . . . . . . . . . . . . 22
The kingdom of God as the all-embracing
rule of God. . . . . . . . . . . . . . . . . . . . . . . . . . . . . . . . . . . . . 23
The Christian idea of sphere-sovereignty over against the
pagan view that the state is related to the other societal structures
as the whole to its parts . . . . . . . . . . . . . . . . . . . . . . . . . . . . . 23

The Roman Catholic view of the Christian state – Thomas Aquinas – is a falling away from the Scriptural conception ................ 24
Infiltration of the pagan totality-idea in the Roman Catholic concept of the church ........................................ 24
A false view of the Christian state: the state is subject to the temporal church-institute .................................... 24
Penetration of this view in modern denominational political parties ...... 24
The Reformation over against the Roman Catholic view of Christian society ........................................... 25
Nominalism in Late-Scholasticism ............................... 25
The nominalistic conception of the law as subjective arbitrariness and the Thomistic idea of the law as rational order ............... 25
The nominalist dualism of nature and grace ....................... 26
This dualism was perpetuated in Luther's law-gospel polarity .......... 27
Melanchthon's synthesis ...................................... 27
Brunner continues Luther's dualism .............................. 27
Calvin breaks with the dualistic nature-grace scheme ................ 28
Calvin's Scriptural view of law ................................. 28
The law as boundary between God and creature ................... 29
Calvin's view of the divine creation-order contrasted with Thomas Aquinas . 29
The principle of sphere-sovereignty: Calvin and Althusius ............ 29
The greater influence of Melanchthon's synthesis predominates ........ 30
The rise of the modern humanistic world- and life-view .............. 30
The overpowering influence of the new mathematical science-ideal upon modern culture ......................................... 30
The humanistic ideal of science continues in the modern individualistic idea of the state ............................................ 31
Relativizing character of modern individualism in its view of society ..... 31
Humanistic natural law over against its Aristotelian-Thomistic counterpart .. 32
Two mainstreams in humanistic natural law and the idea of the *Rechtsstaat* in its first phase of development .................. 32
The old-liberal view of the *Rechtsstaat* and the separation of Church and State ........................................... 32
Tolerance in State-absolutism .................................. 33
The Calvinistic view of sphere-sovereignty has nothing in common with the humanistic freedom-idea of natural law .................. 33
The truly Christian idea of the state cannot be separated from a recognition of sphere-sovereignty ............................... 34
The radical difference between sphere-sovereignty and autonomy ....... 34
Autonomy is proper only to parts of a whole; sphere-sovereignty does not allow for such a relation ............................... 34
Sphere-sovereignty and antithesis go hand in hand in Kuyper .......... 35
Kuyper broke with nature-grace and distinguished between church as institute and as organism .................................... 35

Elaboration of Kuyper's views the first meaning of sphere-sovereignty,
the sovereign law-spheres . . . . . . . . . . . . . . . . . . . . . . . . . . . . 36
Temporal aspects of reality in distinct law-spheres . . . . . . . . . . . . . . 36
The religious root-unity of the law-spheres . . . . . . . . . . . . . . . . . . . 37
As sunlight diffuses itself in prismatic beauty . . . . . . . . . . . . . . . . . 37
Common grace and the grace of rebirth (*palingenesis*):
no dualistic doctrine . . . . . . . . . . . . . . . . . . . . . . . . . . . . . . . . 37
Sphere-universality of the law-spheres . . . . . . . . . . . . . . . . . . . . . 38
Succession of the law-spheres and the organic character
of sphere-sovereignty . . . . . . . . . . . . . . . . . . . . . . . . . . . . . . . 38
Disclosure and deepening of the meaning of a law-sphere . . . . . . . . . . 39
The second meaning of sphere-sovereignty: individuality-structures
in things and in societal relationships . . . . . . . . . . . . . . . . . . . . . . 39
Concrete things function in all law-spheres indiscriminately.
The significance of the typical qualifying function . . . . . . . . . . . . . . 39
The first meaning of sphere-sovereignty (law-spheres) is not voided
in the individuality-structure of things. The thing as individual totality . . . . . 40
The basic error of humanistic science: the attempt to dissolve the
individuality-structure of a thing in a pattern of lawful relations
within one aspect of reality . . . . . . . . . . . . . . . . . . . . . . . . . . . . 41
The individuality-structure of societal relationships . . . . . . . . . . . . . . 41
The typical founding function . . . . . . . . . . . . . . . . . . . . . . . . . . 41
The structural principle of the state. The state an institution required
because of sin. This Scriptural view not maintained by Thomas Aquinas . . . . 42
One-sided action for national disarmament is a neglect of the
structural principle of the state . . . . . . . . . . . . . . . . . . . . . . . . . . 42
The indissoluble coherence of the typical foundational function and
the typical qualifying function of the state . . . . . . . . . . . . . . . . . . . 43
The "common good" (public welfare) as jural principle and as
absolutistic principle of power . . . . . . . . . . . . . . . . . . . . . . . . . . 43
The old-liberal idea of the *Rechtsstaat* proves powerless to
control the absolutism of "common good" . . . . . . . . . . . . . . . . . . . 44
The humanistic idea of the *Rechtsstaat* in its second, formalistic phase . . . . 44
Only the Christian idea of the state, rooted in the principle
of sphere-sovereignty, is the true idea of the *Rechtsstaat* . . . . . . . . . . . 44
The task of the state cannot be limited externally by excluding
the state from certain aspects of reality . . . . . . . . . . . . . . . . . . . . . 45
The state, with its function as political faith-community,
may not be subjected to an ecclesiastical creed . . . . . . . . . . . . . . . . . 45
Christian faith deepens the typically political principles of justice.
The Roman and the Christian idea of justice . . . . . . . . . . . . . . . . . . 46
The liberal-humanistic and the Fascist views of justice . . . . . . . . . . . . 46
All non-Christian theories of the state are essentially theories of power
(Machtsstaatstheorieen) . . . . . . . . . . . . . . . . . . . . . . . . . . . . . . 47

The true relation of state and church: not a mechanical division,
but sphere-sovereignty. . . . . . . . . . . . . . . . . . . . . . . . . . . . . 47
The inseparable, interwoven texture of the various structures of society . . . . 48
The prophetic task of Christianity in these times . . . . . . . . . . . . . . . . 48

### The relation of the individual and community from a legal philosophical perspective

Individualistic and Universalistic conceptions of Law . . . . . . . . . . . . . 49
Civil Law and the idea of the State . . . . . . . . . . . . . . . . . . . . . . 51
The State as Public Legal Institution . . . . . . . . . . . . . . . . . . . . . 55

### The contest over the concept of sovereignty

Introduction . . . . . . . . . . . . . . . . . . . . . . . . . . . . . . . . . . 57
The History of the Dogma. . . . . . . . . . . . . . . . . . . . . . . . . . . . 58
    Bodin's concept of sovereignty and the humanistic doctrine
    of natural law . . . . . . . . . . . . . . . . . . . . . . . . . . . . . . . 58
    The historical interpretation of the concept of sovereignty and
    the doctrine of state-sovereignty . . . . . . . . . . . . . . . . . . . . . . 63
    The doctrine of the sovereignty of law (Rechtssouveranität) and
    its presumed victory over the traditional dogma of sovereignty. . . . . . . 68
The traditional concept of sovereignty and the
doctrine of sovereignty in its proper orbit . . . . . . . . . . . . . . . . . . . 69

### Selections from A New Critique of Theoretical Thought on the State

The empirical data concerning the State's character . . . . . . . . . . . . 75
The typical foundational function of the State . . . . . . . . . . . . . . . 76
The myth of blood-relationship in the German national-socialistic
ideology of the "third Empire," and the typical foundational function
in the structure of the State . . . . . . . . . . . . . . . . . . . . . . . . . 77
The fundamental error of considering all different forms of power
intrinsically equivalent components of the power of the State . . . . . . . 79
The invariable character of the foundational function in the structure
of the State. . . . . . . . . . . . . . . . . . . . . . . . . . . . . . . . . . . 80
The structural subject-object relation in the monopolistic organization
of military power over a territorial cultural area . . . . . . . . . . . . . . 82
The levelling constructive schema of the whole and its parts
confronted with the fourfold use of a fruitful idea of totality . . . . . . . . 82

### THE TYPICAL LEADING FUNCTION OF THE STATE AND THE THEORY OF THE SO-CALLED 'PURPOSES' OF THE BODY POLITIC

The theories of the "purposes of the State" bear no reference to the
internal structural principle of the body politic . . . . . . . . . . . . . . . 84
The old liberal theory of the law-State as a theory of the purpose
of the body politic. . . . . . . . . . . . . . . . . . . . . . . . . . . . . . . 84

The theory of the law-State in its second phase as the theory of the merely formal limitation of the purposes of the State. The formalistic conception of administrative jurisdiction . . . . . . . . . . . . . . . . . . 86
The third phase in the development of the theory of the law-State. The uselessness of any attempt to indicate fundamental external limits to the State's task by the construction of limited subjective purposes of the body politic . . . . . . . . . . . . . . . . . . . . . . . . . 88
The typical leading function of the State in its indissoluble coherence with its foundational function . . . . . . . . . . . . . . . . . . 90
The typical integrating character of the leading legal function in the structure of the State. The State's people as an integrated whole . . . . 92
The real structure of the internal public law. In the monistic legal theories this structure is ignored and an unjustified appeal is made to legal history. . . . . . . . . . . . . . . . . . . . . . . . . . . . . . . . . . 94
The real meaning of the absolutist idea of the State and the true idea of the law-State. . . . . . . . . . . . . . . . . . . . . . . . . . . . . . . 96
The idea of "the public interest" and the internal limits set to it by the structural principle of the State. . . . . . . . . . . . . . . . . . . . 97
The *salus publica* and distributive justice . . . . . . . . . . . . . . . . 99
The civil law-sphere of the State . . . . . . . . . . . . . . . . . . . . . . 100
The inner nature of the Roman ius gentium . . . . . . . . . . . . . . . 102
The radical difference between common private law and the undifferentiated popular or tribal law . . . . . . . . . . . . . . . . . . . 103

## Political Theories of the Modern Age

State Absolutism . . . . . . . . . . . . . . . . . . . . . . . . . . . . . . . . . . . . 105
Critical Turning Point . . . . . . . . . . . . . . . . . . . . . . . . . . . . . . . . 107
Classical Liberalism . . . . . . . . . . . . . . . . . . . . . . . . . . . . . . . . . 110
Radical Democracy . . . . . . . . . . . . . . . . . . . . . . . . . . . . . . . . . 115

## Glossary

. . . . . . . . . . . . . . . . . . . . . . . . . . . . . . . . . . . . . . . . . . . . . . . 119

## Index

. . . . . . . . . . . . . . . . . . . . . . . . . . . . . . . . . . . . . . . . . . . . . . . 129

# Introductory Essay

David T. Koyzis
Redeemer College
Ancaster, Ontario, Canada

# Political theory in the Calvinist tradition

It is probably fair to say that, until recently, political theory in the Reformed Calvinistic tradition was largely unknown in the mainstream of academia. Where it was known, its character and impact were often subject to misinterpretation. For example, George Sabine discusses Calvinism very largely in the context of the seventeenth-century controversies over the right of popular revolt against tyranny.[1] Quentin Skinner takes a similar approach,[2] although both he and Sabine acknowledge that Calvin's own views on the matter were more nuanced than those of his followers. Others, from sociologist Max Weber (1864-1920) to economist R.H. Tawney (1880-1962), have sought to demonstrate a connection between the teachings of Calvin and his followers and the later development of industrial capitalism in the west.[3] Canadian philosopher George Parkin Grant (1918-1988) follows in this tradition and sees the motivating "primal" of Calvinism to be bound up with liberalism and its attendant emphasis on technical mastery of the physical environment. For Grant the Calvinist impetus is inexorably activistic and has little patience for theory and contemplation of any sort, whether political or otherwise.[4]

Many observers tend to make one of two errors in their assessment of Calvinism as such. The first is to identify it almost wholly with the doctrine of predestination, despite the fact that this preoccupation arose only in the century after the Reformation. The second is to assume that, while Calvinism does have political significance, it is limited to being a kind of precursor to classical liberalism and the modern industrial society. Yet the more astute observers have understood that something more is to be found in this tradition. Philoso-

---

1  George Sabine and Thomas L. Thorson, A History of Political Theory (Hinsdale, Illinois: The Dryden Press, 1973, 4th ed.), pp.339 ff, 352 ff.

2  Quentin Skinner, *The Foundations of Modern Political Thought: Volume Two: The Age of the Reformation* (Cambridge: Cambridge University Press, 1978), pp.189 ff.

3  Max Weber, *The Protestant Ethic and the Spirit of Capitalism* (New York: Charles Scribner's Sons, 1958); and R.H. Tawney, *Religion and the Rise of Capitalism* (Harcourt, Brace & World, 1926).

4  George Grant, *Technology and Empire: Perspectives on North America* (Toronto: Anansi Press, 1969).

pher Nicholas Wolterstorff correctly argues that Calvinism is a type of "world-formative" Christianity with considerable implications, not only for the personal lives of individual Christians, but for the structures of the larger social world.[1] The Dutch statesman, Abraham Kuyper, described the Calvinist version of Christianity as a "life-system" with relevance, not only to religion, but to the arts, the sciences and politics as well.[2] Even Tawney understood that the Calvinist creed sought "to renew society by penetrating every department of life, public as well as private, with the influence of religion."[3] This was to encompass both politics and the academic study of politics, the latter of which includes what is conventionally labelled political philosophy or theory.

In fact, the Calvinist Reformation spawned a distinctive tradition of political theorizing that finds its culmination in the writings of Herman Dooyeweerd (1894-1977), arguably the most original Christian philosopher of the twentieth century. Calvin himself devoted the last section of his famous *Institutes of the Christian Religion* (book IV, chapter XX) to civil government and its place in God's world. Johannes Althusius (c. 1557-1638), writing at the beginning of the seventeenth century, built on this tradition of political reflection and articulated a theory that can justly be labelled pluralist, in contrast to the mainstream of the tradition extending from Bodin through Hobbes to Rousseau, for which absolute, indivisible sovereignty is deemed an indispensable political principle. Indeed, a primary motive behind the publication of Frederick S. Carney's English translation of Althusius' *Politics*[4] was to demonstrate its influence on the subsequent development of federalism, on later understandings of limited government, and even on the increasing acceptance of popular participation in the political process. Althusius lived in the border regions between Germany and the Netherlands, and it is to the latter that we must go to trace further the development of Calvinist political theory.

By the the beginning of the nineteenth century the secularizing ideas generated by the French Revolution were having a large impact throughout Europe, including the Netherlands. In this context, many Christians were concerned over the future of their faith's public witness in a climate where secularization was increasingly paired with a monolithic understanding of state sovereignty, thereby potentially threatening any communal attempt to live a consistently Christian way of life. The re-establishment of the Netherlands as a highly centralized monarchy after 1815 was a characteristic development in line with this trend. So was the effective nationalization of the *Nederlandsch Hervormde Kerk* (Dutch Reformed Church) by King Willem I.

---

1   Nicholas Wolterstorff, *Until Justice and Peace Embrace* (Grand Rapids: Eerdmans, 1983).
2   Abraham Kuyper, *Lectures on Calvinism* (Grand Rapids: Eerdmans, 1931), originally presented as the Stone Lectures in 1898 at Princeton Seminary.
3   Tawney, p.91.
4   *The Politics of Johannes Althusius* (Boston: Beacon Press, 1964).

Out of the believing Reformed Christian community arose two leaders who would offer some hope for the future. These were Guillaume Groen van Prinsterer (1801-1876) and Abraham Kuyper (1837-1920), who successively led what came to be labelled the anti-revolutionary movement in their country. Groen is best known for his classic *Ongeloof en Revolutie* (*Unbelief and Revolution*), written in 1847, just ahead of the European revolutions of the following year.[1] Although Groen's political thought owed much to the romantic restorationist school that emerged following the defeat of Napoléon, he began to move in a strikingly different direction in his later years, paving the way for Kuyper to assume his mantle of leadership after his death.

Kuyper was an extraordinary figure who seemed uniquely capable of wearing several hats throughout his long public career. He can justly be labelled pastor, theologian, scholar, journalist, educator and statesman. Although he began his career in the parish ministry, he moved on to many other accomplishments. He became editor of both De Standaard and De Heraut, a Christian daily and weekly respectively. He founded the first Dutch political party, the Antirevolutionary Party in 1879, which was also the first Christian Democratic party in the world. The following year he founded the Free University, a Christian university established on Reformed principles. He was first elected to the Second Chamber of the Dutch Parliament in 1874 and eventually served as Prime Minister from 1901 to 1905. Kuyper's thought was introduced to North America in 1898, when he delivered the Stone Lectures at Princeton Seminary.[2]

Although Kuyper was not an academic political theorist, he nevertheless laid the foundations for a highly original approach to politics that would come to be labelled "Kuyperian." Its originality consisted at the outset in the fact that he sought to articulate a consistently Christian view of the place of politics in God's world that would be free from the distortions of various nonchristian ideologies. In this respect he was the heir of Groen's approach in *Unbelief and Revolution*. Yet Kuyper also understood that one cannot simply close the gates around the community of faith and pretend that those outside have nothing to offer. Because of God's common grace (*gemeene gratie*), one can expect even unbelievers to offer fragmentary insights into his world. Kuyper was by no means the first Christian to understand that the sharp antithesis between belief and unbelief by no means precludes a recognition of God's common grace. Augustine himself articulated the same fundamental truth in his *De Civitate Dei*. But Kuyper worked out this understanding at a time when the churches of both Europe and North America were polarizing into the two po-

---

1  See Harry Van Dyke, *Groen van Prinsterer's Lectures on Unbelief and Revolution* (Jordan Station, Ontario: Wedge Publishing Foundation, 1989) for an abridged English translation of this work with an interpretive essay.
2  See Peter S. Heslam, *Creating a Christian Worldview: Abraham Kuyper's Lectures on Calvinism* (Grand Rapids: Eerdmans, 1998).

sitions that H. Richard Niebuhr would come to describe as "Christ against culture" and "Christ of culture," representing conservative and liberalizing tendencies respectively.[1]

The most characteristic feature of Kuyper's political thought is the principle of *soevereiniteit in eigen kring*, usually referred to in English as "sovereignty in its own sphere," "sovereignty in its proper orbit," or simply "sphere sovereignty."[2] Sphere sovereignty implies three things: (1) ultimate sovereignty belongs to God alone; (2) all earthly sovereignties are subordinate to and derivative from God's sovereignty; and (3) there is no mediating earthly sovereignty from which others are derivative. The first two implications serve to distingush Kuyper's theory from those of liberal individualism, in which the individual is seen as sovereign over the array of communities he is supposed to have created, and of the various collectivisms, in which a single overarching community is deemed sovereign over other communities and individuals underneath. The third implication serves to differentiate sphere sovereignty from the principle of subsidiarity, whose roots are in the Roman Catholic tradition and whose conception of society is markedly hierarchical. Much as the Reformation had sought to emphasize the direct, unmediated access of Christians to God, so also Kuyper's principle pointed to the direct, unmediated authority conferred by God on the various societal forms that have emerged over the course of history.

However, two problems arise out of Kuyper's conception of sphere sovereignty, one of which is terminological and the other of which is more ontological in character. First, many observers are less than fully happy with Kuyper's use of the word "sovereignty" in this context. For most English-speakers sovereignty has clear connotations of absolute power unchecked by anything or anyone outside of itself. In Hobbes' *Leviathan*, for example, the sovereign stands above the compact and is not bound by its terms. In the United Kingdom parliamentary sovereignty means that Parliament can act without fear of intervention by a court authorized to rule on the constitutionality of one of its acts. Sovereignty means to have the last word, the final say, the ultimate authority. If this is so, then it is by no means appropriate to assign such a quality to mere human beings, whose range and scope of legitimate action are always limited in some fashion.

For this reason more recent theorists in the Kuyperian tradition prefer to speak of "differentiated authority" or even "differentiated responsibility," the latter of which is perhaps better able to capture, in addition to the authority of communities, the legitimate freedom of the individual within the larger social con-

---

1  H. Richard Niebuhr, *Christ and Culture* (New York: Harper & Brothers, 1951).
2  See Kuyper, "The Antirevolutionary Program," James W. Skillen and Rockne M McCarthy, ed., *Political Order and the Plural Structure of Society* (Atlanta: Scholar's Press, 1991), especially pp.257 ff.

text.¹ Yet whether one uses sovereignty, authority or responsibility, the assumption undergirding the Kuyperian approach is that society is multiform and consists of a variety of responsible agents, both communal and individual, whose legitimate range of activity is rooted immediately in God's sovereignty and which exist within normative limits placed on them by God himself.

The second and more serious difficulty with Kuyper's conception of sphere sovereignty is that, while it has a solid intuitive basis in actual human experience, it lacks a certain theoretical sophistication. Why, one might ask, does the state constitute a sphere distinct from that of, say, the institutional church? Why ought parents to possess the responsibility of disciplining their own children? Why should they not call in a police officer instead? Why, further, should not business enterprises and labour unions become arms of the state? To be sure, Kuyper could answer that these spheres normatively remain distinct because of God's creation ordinances. His answer would be correct, but in itself it would not take us very far in our attempts to understand which areas of life are distinct spheres and which are not.

For example, if a federal constitution grants exclusive jurisdiction over education to the state or provincial governments, is a subsequent federal intervention in this field a violation of sphere sovereignty? Or is it merely a possible infringement of a right under positive law requiring adjudication by a constitutional court? Is a distinct ethnic, cultural or racial community a sphere in Kuyper's sense? Does racial intermarriage constitute a violation of sphere sovereignty? These are, of course, no mere hypothetical questions, because they were discussed in South Africa during the years that the apartheid policy was being conceived and implemented. If church and state are distinct spheres, but federal and provincial governments and Ukrainian and Polish ethnic communities are not, we must find some way to account theoretically for our different assessment of these pairs.

### Dooyeweerd's unique contribution

Here is where Dooyeweerd enters the picture. After Kuyper's death in 1920 it fell to Dooyeweerd to develop further, with a higher degree of theoretical consistency and sophistication, the insights articulated in only seminal fashion by the former.² Having grown up in the Reformed Christian community in the

---

1 To understand better the meaning and implications of differentiated responsibility, see James W. Skillen, *The Scattered Voice: Christians at Odds in the Public Square* (Grand Rapids: Zondervan, 1990), and *Recharging the American Experiment: Principled Pluralism for Genuine Civic Community* (Grand Rapids: Baker Books, 1994); and Paul Marshall, "Politics Not Ethics: A Christian Perspective on the State," *Servant or Tyrant: The Task and Limits of Government* (Mississauga, Ontario: Christian Labour Association of Canada and Work Research Foundation, 1989), pp.5-24.

2 For more detailed accounts of Dooyeweerd's activities and influence, see Bernard Zylstra's introduction to L. Kalsbeek, *Contours of a Christian Philosophy: An introduction to Herman Dooyeweerd's thought* (Toronto: Wedge, 1975), pp.14-33; and Albert M. Wolters, "The Intellectual Milieu of Herman Dooyeweerd," C.T. MacIntire, ed., *The Legacy of Herman Dooyeweerd: Reflections on critical philosophy in the Christian Tradition* (Lanham, Maryland: University Press of America, 1985), pp.1-19.

Netherlands, Dooyeweerd studied law at the Free University where he earned his doctorate in 1917. In 1922 he became director of the Kuyper Institute in The Hague. Then from 1926 until his retirement in 1965, he taught at the Free University. He was a prolific scholar who wrote a large number of publications, culminating in 1935 with his massive three-volume work, *De Wijsbegeerte der Wetsidee*,[1] whose title was thereafter associated with the philosophical movement as a whole. The fact that he wrote largely in the Dutch language initially delayed the wider dissemination of his thought. But some twenty years later his 1935 work was translated into English, revised and given the title, *A New Critique of Theoretical Thought*.[2] The present volume is part of a series intended to make the remainder of Dooyeweerd's works accessible to the English-speaking world and beyond.

With respect to his philosophy in general, Dooyeweerd has made at least two unique contributions. To begin with, he has developed a systematic philosophy rooted in the conviction that all theoretical thought has pre-theoretical and nonfalsifiable religious underpinnings.[3] Any theory making a pretence to religious neutrality, whether on the grounds of a universal rational faculty within the person or on the basis of the objective nature of so-called facts in the surrounding world, must be seen for what it is: epistemologically naïve and unaware of its own dogmatic starting point. It is further rooted in a deficient anthropology that elevates one aspect of the total person and makes this the unifying factor of the human self. Yet far from being an apparently neutral faculty, reason can be understood, according to Dooyeweerd, only as the logical aspect of our total experience. In this respect, faith and reason are not the dialectical polarities that much of the western intellectual tradition, from Averroës and Thomas Aquinas to Hobbes and Marx, has come to think of them. Rather they are two aspects of a much richer and fuller human experience. Any effort to account theoretically for this experience is necessarily dependent on an ultimate religious commitment lying outside of and preceding the theoretical enterprise. Even the behavioural political scientist anchors her endeavour in religious convictions concerning the nature of humanity, of the world we inhabit, and of the place of politics in that world.

In the second place, Dooyeweerd's philosophy eschews all reductionisms. Although this principled antireductionism is by no means peculiar to Dooyeweerd, his own contribution consists in (1) his placing this insight within the larger understanding that God's creation is not a haphazard product of chance, but an orderly cosmos subject to norms given by his grace; and (2) his effort to spell out those aspects of reality that are themselves irreducible but, if placed in an apostate religious context, nevertheless lend a certain plausibility to the reductionist project. These irreducible aspects of reality are called *modes*, and the mature Dooyeweerd posits fifteen of these, listed here

---

1  Dooyeweerd, *De Wijsbegeerte der Wetsidee* (Amsterdam: H.J. Paris, 1935-36).

2  Dooyeweerd, *A New Critique of Theoretical Thought* (Amsterdam: H.J. Paris; Philadelphia: Presbyterian and Reformed, 1953-58).

3  See Dooyeweerd, *In the Twilight of Western Thought: Studies in the Pretended Autonomy of Philosophical Thought* (Nutley, New Jersey: The Craig Press, 1960).

in ascending order: arithmetic (number), spatial, kinematic (extensive movement), physical (energy), biotic (organic life), psychic (feeling, sensation), logical, historical (cultural, formative), lingual (symbolic), social, economic, aesthetic, juridical (justice, retribution), ethical (temporal love, loyalty) and pistical (faith). The persistent tendency of nonchristian – or perhaps nontheistic – theoretical thought is, not only to fasten onto one or more of these modal aspects and to read the rest of creation through them, but to assume that doing so provides the key to understanding the world in its totality.

The difficulty with engaging one of these reductionisms in dialogue is due, not to the supposed irrationality of the reductionist, but to the fact that her enterprise accounts for all the evidence in a way that seems to be complete but is nevertheless missing something rather crucial. The convinced materialist can easily explain such complex phenomena as anger or even romantic affection by pointing to the movement of electrical impulses through the brain.[1] In this respect, the materialist is similar to G.K. Chesterton's "madman," who reasons in a way that combines logical completeness with spiritual contraction.[2] If the madman argues that there is a universal conspiracy against him, and if you point out that everyone denies it, he is likely to reply that denial is exactly what one can expect from conspirators. "His explanation covers the facts as much as yours."[3] As Chesterton memorably concludes, the madman is not the one who has lost his reason, but the one "who has lost everything except his reason."[4] Dooyeweerd would put the matter less colourfully perhaps, but he would agree that the materialist, who sees the entire cosmos through the narrow lenses of only one or two modal aspects, has missed the fulness of human life, if not experientially, at least theoretically.

## Politics and the state

Dooyeweerd also brings into his specifically political theory these fundamental insights into the nature of theoretical thought. If reductionism is a danger in unbelieving philosophy in general, it is a continuing threat to our ability to make sense of the political realm as well. Indeed the most influential political theorists in the modern West have in some fashion attempted to reduce politics to something else. The most common error in this respect is to collapse politics into economics.

---

1  Ernst Lubitsch's classic 1939 film, "Ninotchka," plays with the materialism of a stereotypical Soviet functionary to humorous effect. To Melvyn Douglas' flirtatious gestures, Greta Garbo's Russian character replies: "Why must you bring in the wrong values? Love is a romantic designation for a most ordinary biological – or, shall we say, chemical? – process. A lot of nonsense is written about it." To his continued professions of affection, she replies with clinical dispassion: "Chemically, we're already quite sympathetic" (http://www.filmsite.org/nino.html), last modified 21 April 1998, quoting the script by Melchior Lengyel, Charles Brackett, Billy Wilder and Walter Reisch).

2  G.K. Chesterton, *Orthodoxy* (Wheaton, Illinois: Harold Shaw Publishers, 1994), especially pp.9 ff.

3  Chesterton, p.15.

4  *Ibid*.

For example, John Locke argued that virtually the sole *raison d'être* of civil government is the protection of private property. More recent libertarians, such as F.A. von Hayek (1899-1992)[1] and Milton Friedman (1912- ),[2] follow Locke in assuming that life revolves around the marketplace and that government is at best a necessary evil charged with the sole task of setting up procedural rules to stabilize its functioning. Even later liberals less enamoured of the economic market nevertheless tend to speak of a market-place of ideas, as if their truth or falsehood is somehow dependent on the likes and dislikes of their would-be consumers.

Although Karl Marx and his followers can hardly be considered disciples of Locke, they are nevertheless his spiritual heirs to no small extent. For Marx politics is still reducible to economics, though in a rather different sense than for Locke. According to the former, virtually the whole of life can be seen as a series of epiphenomenal outgrowths of the concrete processes of production. Everything that appears to be noneconomic in nature is therefore qualified with a series of "merelys," "no-more-thans" and "nothing-buts" that supposedly bring us closer to an underlying material reality. If Plato believed that the sensible world is less real than the intelligible world, Marx believes, to the contrary, that ideas are less real than the economic arrangements they reflect and the class conflicts that grow out of them. Thus "Political power, properly so called, is merely the organized power of one class for oppressing another."[3] The expectation is that, with the eventual end of the class struggle, there will be little or no need for the state as we now know it. In the words of Marx and Engels, "the public power will lose its political character." Engels by himself is even more explicit: the state will "wither away."

In a somewhat different though related vein, the American political scientist, David Easton (1917- ), describes politics as "the authoritative allocation of values for a whole society."[4] Similarly, Harold Lasswell (1902- ) sees politics as basically a distributive process deciding "who gets what, when, how."[5] Although such definitions have a certain plausibility to them, they too are unable adequately to distinguish politics from other fields of human endeavour, especially economics. The irony is that, although such accounts of politics are close to the centre of the discipline of political science, particularly in the United States, in the real world of the academy political scientists have little difficulty knowing intuitively what they are expected to study. Thus the field may be somewhat less fragmented than the diversity of definitions would

---

1   See F.A. von Hayek, *The Road to Serfdom* (Chicago: University of Chicago Press, 1944).
2   See Milton Friedman, *Capitalism and Freedom* (Chicago: University of Chicago Press, 1962); and, with Rose Friedman, *Free to Choose* (New York: Harcourt Brace Jovanovich, 1980).
3   Karl Marx and Friedrich Engels, *The Manifesto of the Communist Party* (1848).
4   David Easton, *A Systems Analysis of Political Life* (New York: Wiley, 1965).
5   Harold Lasswell, *Politics: Who Gets What, When, How* (New York: Meridian Books, 1958).

seem to suggest.¹

Even such Christian political theorists as Jacques Ellul (1912-1994) and George Grant have not avoided falling into their own brands of reductionism. Although each in his own way is severely critical of the major traditions of liberalism and socialism so influential in the past two centuries, both effectively reduce politics to some nonpolitical factor. For Ellul the state and its activities are caught up in a grand process of technological expansion that is effectively autonomous and thus virtually immune to human control and responsibility.² Grant is largely in agreement with Ellul and, connecting technique with the economic forces of capitalism, believes that continental economic integration must of necessity lead to political amalgamation.³

In recent years, however, we have witnessed something of a countermovement to the above-mentioned reductionisms, and it is useful to look at Dooyeweerd in this larger context.

We might begin with Hannah Arendt (1906-1975), who is preoccupied with the recovery of politics in a world obsessed with the imposition of single-minded ideological projects. Above all, Arendt seeks to protect the public realm as a space for genuine human freedom, where citizens might come together to act and speak in the presence of their fellow citizens. Any movement that would deny what she labels the human condition of plurality risks putting an end to genuine politics and replacing it with something nonpolitical.⁴ Like Ellul and Grant, Arendt too fears the monism implicit in technique, but she cannot share her contemporaries' fatalism in believing in technique's inevitable triumph over politics.

Arendt's influence can be detected in the writings of Bernard Crick (1929- ), particularly his classic *In Defence of Politics*.⁵ Crick agrees with her that politics "is not religion, ethics, law, science, history, or economics,"⁶ but is a distinctive activity in its own right operating in accordance with its own imperatives. Rooted in the fact of human diversity – of the existence of different groups, interests, traditions, even truths – politics necessitates the willingness

---

1  For an excellent survey and analysis of the discipline of political science, see James W. Skillen, "Toward a Comprehensive Science of Politics," Jonathan Chaplin and Paul Marshall, ed., *Political Theory and Christian Vision: Essays in Memory of Bernard Zylstra* (Lanham, Maryland: University Press of America, 1994), pp.57 ff.

2  Ellul's writings are too numerous to list in full. Among his better known works are *The Technological Society* (New York: Alfred Knopf, 1964) and *The Political Illusion* (New York: Alfred Knopf, 1967). See also *The Technological System* (New York: Seabury, 1980).

3  See Grant's argument in *Lament for a Nation: The Defeat of Canadian Nationalism* (Toronto: McClelland and Stewart, 1965), concerning the fate of Canada in an American-dominated North American economy. Although the rise of NAFTA and the European Union might seem on the surface to vindicate his fears, it is telling that, at the precise moment continental economic integration is occurring, separatist movements, such as those in Québec, Scotland and Kosovo are also making their impact in these same regions.

4  Hannah Arendt, *The Human Condition* (Chicago: University of Chicago Press, 1958).

5  Fourth edition (London: Weidenfeld & Nicolson, 1992), first published in 1962.

6  Crick, p.15.

of all parties to compromise and to accept less than they might prefer to claim from the political process. Politics, in short, is the peaceful conciliation of diversity, a way of settling conflicts before they escalate into overt violence. Crick is at pains to defend politics – however precarious and untidy it may seem to those of a more dogmatic bent – from all who would impose their single idea of the common good on a diverse society.

In similar fashion, Sheldon S. Wolin argues that politics is an activity centred on group competition amid conditions of change and relative scarcity whose consequences affect an entire society.[1] Political community is distinct from other communities insofar as it is uniquely concerned with that which is common to the whole of society. Such concerns include "national defense, internal order, the dispensing of justice, and economic regulation."[2] However, the modern world has been characterized by the sublimation of politics and its replacement by an ethos of organization. This ethos is characterized by the ongoing effort to uncover scientific laws to which social phenomena might be subjected in the interest of scientific truth. Freedom and citizenship are thus deprecated in favour of order, structure and regularity.[3]

We could continue this brief survey and look at Leo Strauss[4] (1899-1973), Eric Voegelin[5] (1901-1985), Jean Bethke Elshtain[6] (1941- ) and many others. Each in his or her own way attempts to underscore the distinctiveness of politics in opposition to those who would, even inadvertently, reduce it to something else of a nonpolitical character. Most do so by speaking of such things as diversity, plurality, public freedom, common interest and the like. But even these factors are not sufficient to delimit politics as a unique enterprise since they can be found in a variety of contexts, ranging from business enterprises to ecclesiastical settings.

Here is where Dooyeweerd makes his singular contribution to an understanding of what is and is not political. Indeed Dooyeweerd rarely uses the adjective "political" without it qualifying some noun, as in, for example, "political community." This already gives us a strong indication of Dooyeweerd's approach. For what distinguishes politics proper from what many are wont to call church politics, office politics and school politics is that the former occurs within the context of a particular community known as the state. In Kuyper's view the state is one of the spheres to which a limited, differentiated share of human sovereignty is ascribed. But how can we know this? What differentiates the state from the church, the corporation, the private club, the school, the labour union? Once more we are capable of intuiting the difference without

---

1  Sheldon S. Wolin, *Politics and Vision: Continuity and Innovation in Western Political Thought* (Boston: Little, Brown and Company, 1960), pp.10-11.

2  Wolin, pp.2-3.

3  Wolin, pp.352 ff.

4  See, for example, Leo Strauss, *What Is Political Philosophy? and Other Studies* (Westport, Connecticut: Greenwood Press, 1959), and particularly the title essay.

5  See Eric Voegelin, *The New Science of Politics* (Chicago: University of Chicago Press, 1952), and *Science, Politics and Gnosticism* (Chicago: Regnery Gateway, 1968).

6  See especially Jean Bethke Elshtain, *Democracy on Trial* (New York: Basic Books, 1995).

necessarily being able to account for this theoretically. Nevertheless, accounting for it theoretically helps to enrich our intuitive experience of reality and it furthermore helps to confirm or discount our hunches.

Dooyeweerd believes we can account for the state's uniqueness by analyzing what he calls its "structural principle." This is the subject of the first essay in this volume. Following Kuyper, Dooyeweerd's vision of society is one in which different God-given norms operate in distinct spheres of human responsibility. One of the principal norms governing the process of historical development is that of societal differentiation. In undifferentiated communities a number of functions related to its ongoing existence are concentrated in a few hands. In such contexts a chieftain is at once political leader, cultic religious leader, head of a clan or kinship community and so forth. But as the society develops and becomes more complex, these functions come to be performed by distinct communities and institutions defined in some sense by these functions. Thus, whereas at one time the family was simultaneously a biological, economic and educational unit, the process of differentiation eventually led to the formation of economic enterprises and schools distinct from the family unit. In similar fashion, though at one time cultic religious functions and political functions were often combined in the same institution, differentiation has led to the separation of these into distinct church and state institutions. In a mature, differentiated society, each of these institutions is subject to specific creational norms governing its activities and rooted in a relationship between two of the modal aspects, as we shall further explain below.

*Power and justice: transcending another false polarity*
Even among those theorists who understand that politics has something to do with power and justice – or with what Dooyeweerd labels the historical and juridical modalities respectively – there is a persistent tendency to play these two aspects off against each other as though they were, once again, polarities. Much as the mainstream of the western intellectual tradition has perceived a dialectical relationship between faith and reason, so has it struggled to articulate a theory of political community and governmental authority within the context of a dialectical interplay between power and justice.

Political realists, for example, are quite willing to admit that politics has to do with power. Hans Morgenthau, perhaps the greatest twentieth-century proponent of this position, is easily able to see that politics ought not to be confused with, or reduced to, other activities, including economics. Yet he is unable to see that justice is a norm with any relevance to politics. Justice is properly confined to the realm of personal morality, and one cannot reasonably expect of a state what one can of an individual person. Hence the overriding norm for political action is not justice, but a prudence that judges political decisions in accordance with the norm of success in achieving goals. Consequences are all-important for the political realist.[1] Morgenthau stands in the tradition of Augustine, who also deemed it necessary, for apparently solid empirical rea-

---

[1] Hans Morgenthau, *Politics Among Nations* (New York: Alfred A. Knopf, 1948).

POLITICAL PHILOSOPHY

sons, to abandon justice as a defining feature of the commonwealth.[1] However, like Augustine and his political realist successors, even Morgenthau is not willing to allow power to remain unguided by some norm. Peace and stability are all-important to political realists, but they are unable to see that these might be significant elements of justice itself.

Not all political realists are enthusiasts for power, however, and this brings something of a paradoxical quality to their enterprise. For example, Lord Acton famously argues that power corrupts. Glenn Tinder further notes the "moral dubiousness" of power and admits that it may even be "evil in essence."[2] From Dooyeweerd's perspective, such observations effectively ontologize evil by ascribing it, not to human disobedience to God's will, but to something in the very structure of creation itself.[3] Other realists, such as Reinhold Niebuhr, are willing to admit that power itself is not evil, though it is continually in danger of fostering evil if it is not hedged about with effective limitations rooted in a balance of competing powers.[4] Indeed, the moment of truth in the political realist position stems from its understanding that all human power must be contained within such limits.

Where political realism errs, however, is in its somewhat facile assumption that all power is simply self-interested and undifferentiated. We begin with self-interest. At first blush, it would seem safer to assume, along Hobbesian lines, that our fellow human beings are out to get us than to expect them to act beneficently towards us. Indeed, it would be unwise to imagine that no one is willing to harm us, and for this reason many people quite sensibly lock their doors at night as a precaution. However, our own experience of life does not vindicate the worst fears of a Hobbes. Parental authority, for example, is not simply exercised in the self-interest of the parents but in the interest of the children. As even Plato understood, if political power were exercised only in the interest of rulers, it would not be necessary to compensate them for the inconvenience of ruling. To be sure, parents and rulers sometimes abuse their respective offices, but doing so constitutes a perversion of the norm. In short, power is capable of being abused, but this abuse is the perversion of something good.

---

1  Augustine tested Cicero's definition of a *res publica* as a community bound together by ties of justice and found it wanting. After all, he reasoned, the old Roman republic was certainly a *res publica*, yet, by withholding from God the worship due him, it was lacking in justice. Thus if a known *res publica* lacks justice, we must exclude justice from any empirical definition of this phenomenon (*De Civitate Dei*, XIX, 21). The flaw in Augustine's reasoning comes from his failure to understand the modal juridical character of the *res publica* and his concomitant tendency instead to view justice as a substantial entity that is either present *in toto* or absent *in toto*.

2  Glenn Tinder, Political Thinking: *The Perennial Questions*, 5th ed. (New York: Harper Collins, 1991), p.95.

3  For a lucid, nontechnical discussion of the distinction between creation structure and spiritual direction, see Albert M. Wolters, *Creation Regained: Biblical Basics for a Reformational Worldview* (Grand Rapids: Eerdmans, 1985).

4  Reinhold Niebuhr, *The Nature and Destiny of Man, vol. II, Human Destiny* (New York: Scribners, 1943), p.22.

Nor is power an undifferentiated human capacity, as the realists further tend to assume. For example, although Stephen Charles Mott understands that power is a good capable of being abused, he is able only to discern what he labels defensive, exploitive and intervening powers.[1] He is less able to account for authority in its legitimate and pluriform manifestations throughout the broad array of human communities.[2] Parental authority is much more than raw, arbitrary power, being inextricably linked, as it is, to the raising of children. Magisterial authority is distinguished from political authority insofar as the former is intrinsically related to the educational task of the teacher in the school. Political authority is obviously different from other forms of authority, as we can already sense at an intuitive level. However, political realism is incapable of making sense of this difference, because of its tendency to see power as an undifferentiated capacity to make things happen. Mott comes close to understanding the nature of at least political authority in his account of an intervening power acting to restore some sort of missing balance.[3] Even Morgenthau and Niebuhr understand the language of "balance of powers," which they apply in both domestic and international arenas. In other words, even if political realists eschew talk of justice as subjective and moralistic, their need to distinguish state and government from other communities inevitably pushes them in the direction of acknowledging something like justice, which finds its way in, as it were, through the back door.

Once again, the singular virtue of Dooyeweerd's political theory is that it can account for both power and justice as indispensable and complementary elements in understanding the nature of the state and of governing authority within the state. In this respect, Dooyeweerd's approach is better rooted in empirical reality than that of political realism. Like faith and reason, power and justice are not entities in themselves co-existing in dialectical tension. Rather they are integral aspects – *modal* aspects, in Dooyeweerd's language – of a larger reality that must be acknowledged to be complementary and not antithetical to each other. Every entity, including human communities, is characterized by a peculiar relationship between two interrelated modal aspects which Dooyeweerd labels *founding* and *leading* or *qualifying* functions. The qualifying function is "the ultimate functional point of reference for the entire internal structural coherence of the individual whole in the typical groupage

---

1  See Stephen Charles Mott, *A Christian Perspective on Political Thought* (Oxford: Oxford University Press, 1993), esp.pp.13 ff.

2  The very word "authority" occurs on only two pages in his book, pp.61 and 192, as revealed in the index. There is, in fact, a central contradiction in his account of authority. On the one hand, he admits that "Authority, corporate responsibility, and collective decision making are essential to every form of human life" (p.61), which implies a creational basis for authority. Yet on the other hand, he argues that "Authority means that power is voluntarily granted to an actor by the subjects for purposes supported by their values" (*Ibid.*), which implies that authority might perhaps be dispensed with if the will of the subjects is not so inclined. To be sure, consent of the subjects is a necessary component of authority, but authority itself cannot be reduced to such consent.

3  To be fair, although Mott is influenced by the Niebuhrian tradition of political realism, he is able to acknowledge the claims of justice and treats this concept repeatedly in his book (pp.74 ff), as does Niebuhr in his own writings. See Niebuhr, especially pp.244 ff.

of its aspects"[1]. In other words, it is that function which most specifically characterizes the unique structure of an entity and already points us to its unique internal task.

Dooyeweerd does not define founding function explicitly, but illustrates its meaning through a number of examples. L. Kalsbeek describes it as the "lower of the two modalities which characterize certain types of structural wholes."[2] The founding function may also be defined as that modal aspect at which point an entity begins to take on its unique character as a particular entity – or perhaps the modal point at which something begins to be differentiated from other entities at a basic level. States, universities, orchestras, professional associations, fraternal societies and charitable organizations all share the same founding historical function but have different qualifying functions.

On the other hand, parliaments, cabinets, government departments, courts, and regulatory agencies share both founding and qualifying functions, which indicates that they are manifestations of the larger category of *state*, or political community. Among these entities there can be no relation of sphere sovereignty as such; rather the relationships among what are commonly labelled the "branches" of government are subject to positive legal arrangements of a constitutional nature which properly differ from one country to the next. Thus whether a country is governed by an American-style separation of powers or by a more British form of responsible government is not an issue of maintaining versus departing from sphere sovereignty, but of prudential considerations rooted in the unique traditions of a particular political community.

The graph on page 127 illustrates Dooyeweerd's understanding of created reality.

How does Dooyeweerd's structural analysis serve to improve on the approach of, say, political realism? Using Dooyeweerd's language, political realists are able to account only for the founding function of the state, which is in the historical mode – that mode having to do with technique and cultural-formative power. Because state, institutional church, political party and business enterprise are all alike brought into being through human formative power, political realism is unable adequately to distinguish them from each other because it fails to discern their typical leading functions. Once again, at a pretheoretical experiential level we can easily tell the differences among these institutions. Dooyeweerd's theory thus accounts for this reality better than the various forms of political realism. It also serves to flesh out theoretically Kuyper's principle of sphere sovereignty by answering the questions posed above as to what does and does not constitute a sovereign sphere.

What is the state then? Dooyeweerd defines it at its foundational level as "an internal monopolistic organization of the power of the sword over a particular cultural area within territorial boundaries."[3] But this swordpower is always inextricably tied to the state's character as "a public legal relationship uniting

---

[1] Dooyeweerd, *New Critique*, III, p.58.

[2] L. Kalsbeek, *Contours of a Christian philosophy: An introduction to Herman Dooyeweerd's thought* (Toronto: Wedge, 1975), p.348.

[3] See p.85 below.

government, people and territory into a politico-juridical whole."[1] This further implies that the state's activity must always be led by its central task of doing justice, that is, of harmonizing the various interests within a territory, weighing their respective claims, and doing so in such a way as to recognize their intrinsic limitations and their proper place within the larger social context. In particular, the state is called upon to interrelate justly the various spheres, ensuring through its coercive power that they do not overreach themselves and encroach upon other legitimate areas of responsibility. In short, justice requires the state to uphold the principle of sphere sovereignty.[2]

There is, of course, much disagreement among political theorists as to whether justice is rooted ultimately in the human will or in something outside of it. Is justice something which takes into account the desires of the members of a community or is it an objective standard whose validity rests in something higher than the community? Justice finds its way into the reflections of a variety of philosophers, ranging from Augustine himself down to John Rawls in our own day. But, predictably, each has articulated a different basis for it, including Plato's forms, Aristotle's virtue, Thomas Aquinas' natural law, Rousseau's general will, and Rawls' pure, self-interested rationality.

From Dooyeweerd's perspective, justice is rooted in a higher standard but it is also rooted in the normal aspirations of a community of persons. On the one hand, Scripture tells us that God himself is a God of justice and commands us to act accordingly.[3] Justice, then, cannot be reduced to mere human preferences. We are not being just simply because we are obeying the laws of the land as expressed by the will of a legislator. Against the likes of Hobbes, who asserts that justice is whatever flows from the lips of the sovereign, we must recognize that positive laws are themselves sometimes unjust. In this respect we must affirm that justice is an objective standard or, better, a creational norm that cannot be reduced to mere human will.

---

1  NC, III, p.437.
2  One might easily ask, of course, what happens when the state itself overreaches its legitimate sphere of responsibility and begins to encroach on the nongovernmental spheres in unwarranted fashion. Dooyeweerd is conspicuously silent on this issue, though one can perhaps posit a possible answer to this thorny question with reference to existing constitutional governments and the mechanisms they employ to prevent this danger. Indeed popular elections held on a regular basis help to maintain government accountability, as do the entrenched laws, ordinary statutes and unwritten conventions that form a country's constitution in the full sense. Writing from within the Roman Catholic neo-Thomist tradition, Yves R. Simon believes that the very existence and vitality of nonstate institutions offer a certain resistance to state absolutism. See Simon, *Philosophy of Democratic Government* (Chicago: University of Chicago Press, 1951), pp.136 ff. Other theorists, from Thomas Aquinas to Calvin and Althusius, believe that a remedy against tyranny might be found in lower magistrates authorized to check the power of a supreme magistrate. This points once again to a constitutional remedy, the precise nature of which would need to be worked out in each polity. It is perhaps not too speculative to assume that Dooyeweerd would likely agree with this general approach.
3  See Jan Dengerink, *The Idea of Justice in Christian Perspective* (Toronto: Wedge, 1978), for a survey of the different notions of justice advanced since the time of Plato.

At the same time, justice cannot be disconnected from human activity, including the normal wishes, aspirations and desires of people. Justice requires human agents both to put it into effect and, as important, to articulate the claims which it attempts to adjudicate. This means that it cannot be conceived as an abstract ideal imposed from on high, but is instead a real response to actual human yearnings, needs and goals. It is this connection with the real world that many "objective" notions of justice are lacking. Justice is not a Platonic idea which we must strive to bring down from heaven to earth. Nor is it rooted in a sort of static nature – even a human nature – antecedent to concrete human beings. Among God's commandments is that to do justice. We are not instructed to struggle to *achieve* justice. We are not to try to *bring it into being*, as if it were a kind of substantial entity that we have to fabricate in accordance with an as yet undetermined blueprint. It is not a goal that we strive to reach, any more than loving our daughters and sons is a kind of vague aspiration for the future. Dooyeweerd's political theory helps us to see that justice, far from being a goal for the future, is an intrinsic aspect – indeed one of the defining features – of the state's structure.

*David Koyzis*
(Redeemer College
Ancaster, ON
Canada L9K 1J4)

# The Christian Idea of The State

TO SPEAK OF "the" Christian idea[2] of the state in the face of the current disparity of thought amongst Christians might seem an audacious undertaking. This may perhaps have been possible during the Middle Ages under the supremacy of the Roman Catholic Church, but surely today's countless schisms within the church and the many different Christian political groups make it seem rather presumptuous, if not far-fetched, to conjecture about one overall Christian Idea of the state.

### Emil Brunner rejects the Christian idea of the state

Even Protestants themselves consider – and always did consider – the idea of a Christian state to be a Roman Catholic fallacy. Emil Brunner, one of the leading figures of the so-called Swiss Theology founded by Barth, made the following cutting statement in his well-known book *Das Gebot und die Ordnungen*[3] (1932): "The Christian state never existed, and it never will." According to him it was precisely one of the fundamental concepts of the Reformation that the state, instituted because of the fall, does not belong to the "Kingdom of Christ," but rather to the natural, secular ordinances. He claims that a Christian state is no more possible than a Christian culture, Christian learning, economy, art, or Christian social action. Brunner views all life in the temporal world, permeated as it is by sin, as belonging to the area of nature. Here "worldly ordinances" are valid. It is the realm of law as loveless rule, from which Christians have been liberated in their inner life of grace, so that they can act in accordance with Christ's command of love of the moment. *Nature* (the realm of temporal world-life outside faith, subject to inflexible "ordinances") and *grace* (the faith-realm of the supra-temporal kingdom of God, subject to the commandment of love which, in the Christian believer, has broken with law and has put it aside [as no longer conceived of] as a universally valid rule), are for Brunner unbridgeably separated. The Roman Catholic Church, he maintains, erred when it propagated the idea of a "Christian world-life" and thus also that of a "Christian state." Such a view, he claims, is

---
1 "The Christian Idea of The State." (*De Christelijke Staatsidee*) Presented at a day for Anti-Revolutionary youth on October 3, 1936 (Apeldoorn, Rotterdam-Utrecht, Libertas-Drukkerijen).
 *Translator:* John Kraay; *Editor:* D.F.M. Strauss.

2 *Editorial note* (DFMS): It may be well to explain the meaning of the term "idea," as it is used by Dooyeweerd. An *idea* represents a way of knowing transcending *conceptual knowledge*. It points beyond a conceptual diversity towards the totality, unity and origin of creation. Ideas explore the anticipatory direction of modal aspects (also called the transcendental direction of time). Cf. *A New Critique of Theoretical Thought*, Vol.II, pp.186 ff.

3 *Translator's note:* English translation: *The Divine Imperative* (1937).

only possible if a temporal church hierarchy can be accepted as ruler of both state and other secular societal relationships – a type of government that the Reformation rejected outright.

### National-Socialism and Fascism and the idea of the Christian state

If we now turn to look at the recently evolved use of the term "Christian state" by National-Socialism and Fascism, the picture of spiritual chaos is complete. For these two bring together in a tempting way both the pagan notion of a total state, embracing all life-spheres, and the Christian concept of solidarity and love to one's neighbor.

Indeed, never did the idea of the Christian state seem more problematic than today!

Add to this that the spiritual chaos of our restless times penetrates alarmingly into our own ranks so that many hardly comprehend what positive power of attraction Calvinistic political principles can have,[1] and one can understand the only partially veiled indifference with which many Christians speak of the "Christian idea of the State."

### The ever new, inspiring idea of the Christian state and the causes of its decline

And yet the idea of the Christian state will not be sidelined as an abstract notion that has "outlived its usefulness," and now belongs to a dead tradition. Rather, it is still a spiritual treasure, ever new, ever living and inspiring, touching the very heart of one's Christian life – a treasure which we must keep at all costs.

The fundamental cause of the inner weakening of Christian political thought, yes, of the entire Christian mode of life among many Christians in our day, lies not so much in external factors but in inner decay, threatening Christianity from the beginning in its positive endeavor regarding culture, learning, political life and social movement. This was also the danger of which Joshua, called by God, warned the Israelites when they had arrived in the promised land, namely, integration with heathen peoples and the search for a compromise between the service of Jehovah and the worship of idols.

As soon as Christianity began to compromise education, culture, and political life with pagan and humanistic philosophy, with its view of state and culture, Christianity's inner strength was broken. At that moment the process of "becoming like unto the world" began, repeatedly arrested through the grace of God by a spiritual *reveil*, a reformation.

### Synthesis and Antithesis

Time and time again such a reformation had to affirm the uncompromising antithesis against the weakening synthesis, the spirit of compromise with the world.

---

[1] *Translator's note:* References to Dutch historical events are omitted in this translation.

Is it possible that after the latest (Calvinistic) *reveil* under the inspiring Kuyper[1] this process has again repeated itself? Did the spirit of synthesis perhaps infiltrate almost unnoticed also in our own circles? Is it true that Calvinism as a cultural and political movement has lost its sharp edges? Did it become fashionable and acceptable to the world because gradually it became identified with liberalism carrying a Christian stamp?

If so, surely it is high time that once again we realize the radical antithesis that separates the Christian idea of the state from all pagan and humanistic views.

## Actually, there is but one radical and Scriptural idea of the Christian state

It is not true that the Christian view of the state is divided into as many interpretations as there are Christian political groups or movements. Rather, these differences are the fruit of the perilous marriage of Christianity with the movements of the age, which arise from the spirit of this world.

The genuinely Christian idea of the state is rooted in the radical, Scriptural view regarding the relationship between the kingdom of God in Christ Jesus and the temporal societal structures, in which God's general or common grace arrests the dry-rot caused by sin. What then, is this view?

## The contrast of "nature" and "grace" is non-Scriptural. Scripture posits the heart as the religious center of human existence

God's Word does not teach us a contrast between "nature" and "grace," that is, between the nature of God's creation and the redemption in Christ Jesus. It teaches only and exclusively the radical, uncompromising antithesis of sin and redemption, of the realm of darkness and the kingdom of God in Christ.

God created humankind in His image. In the heart of humankind, the religious root, the center of its being, God concentrated all of creation toward His service; here He laid the supra-temporal root of all temporal creatures. This human heart, from which according to Scriptures flow the wellsprings of life, transcends all things temporal in the service of God. The whole religious sense (meaning) of God's creation lies in our heart, our entire ego, our complete self. This heart, in which according to the Word eternity has been laid, is the true supra-temporal center of human existence. At the same time it is the creaturely center of all of God's creation. The apostasy of this heart, of this root of creation, necessarily swept with it all temporal creation. In Adam not only all humankind fell, but also that entire temporal cosmos of which humankind was the crowned head. And in Christ, the Word become flesh, the second Covenant Head, God gave the new root of His redeemed creation, in Whom true humanity was implanted through self-surrender, through surrender of the center of existence, the heart.

---

[1] *Translator's note*: Abraham Kuyper, (1837-1920), Christian statesman, founder of the Anti-Revolutionary Party in the Netherlands, founder of the Free University of Amsterdam, and prolific author.

### The pagan view that "reason" is the supra-temporal center of a person's being

Pagan philosophy, however, taught that the nature of a person, and in it the nature of all temporal things, finds its supra-temporal center in "reason." But this "reason" is in reality nothing other than a composite of temporal functions of consciousness, functions of our self, aspects of our heart in the full scriptural sense. Temporal organic-biotic life, feeling, sense of beauty, our function in historical development, in language, in jural and economic life, etc. – all these are also functions of the heart in this sense.

The kingship of humankind in God's undefiled creation did not lie in the "rational-moral" nature of human beings, but in this great mystery: that God concentrated all of His creation in the heart of humankind, in the whole self of a person, and brought creation together in this deeper unity.

The fall, the fundamental separation from God, consisted in this: the human heart rebelled against its divine Origin; humankind thought itself to be something by virtue of itself; humankind sought itself and with that, God, in temporality. This was the idolatry in the apostasy from the true God, as He had revealed Himself in the heart of humankind through His Word.

A manifestation of this apostasy was also the pagan view that natural human existence has its origin in reason as *supposed* supra-temporal center, and that God Himself is the Absolute, that is *idolized*, *Reason* (Aristotle). Sad to say Christian thought has largely taken this over in the area of so-called "natural" knowledge.

### The effects of compromise of Christian and pagan views. The scheme of "nature" and "grace" as a result of this compromise

As soon as Christian thought had compromised with this pagan philosophy, the truly Scriptural relationship between life in the temporal world and the kingdom of God was no longer understood and false philosophical constructions began to obscure the profound clear truth of God's revelation.

The heart was no longer understood in the Scriptural sense because people no longer understood themselves; and they no longer understood themselves because they had obscured the true knowledge of God with an impossible compromise with apostate philosophical speculations. The "heart" became identified with the temporal psychical function, which was considered the stimulant of the will. That is why men of the Middle Ages began to argue the question which in "human" and in "divine" nature has priority: the intellect (reason) or the will, which according to Greek philosophy arises out of the function of feeling. Thus they also construed a false contrast between "nature" and "grace" because "nature" was considered to be the God-created structure of reality as seen in the light of Greek philosophy, and "grace" the supra-temporal revelation of God, including all Christ's redemptive work.

### Thomas Aquinas on human nature. "Nature" as portal of "grace"

Christ, the Word become flesh, was now no longer seen as the New Root of the order of creation, as the Rectifier of true nature. "Nature," concentrated in "reason," was declared self-sufficient and autonomous in her own area, the temporal world-order. Thomas Aquinas, prince of Roman Catholic Scholasticism, made natural reason independent of the revelation of God in Christ Jesus. Learning, morality, political life, and "natural theology" were then, as autonomous areas of natural reason, practiced in a pagan-Aristotelian manner. But in addition to this intrinsically pagan idea of "nature," a "supra-temporal" area of grace was construed which transcends natural reason and can only be apprehended by the light of God's revelation. "Nature" was made a lower autonomous portal of "grace," and the latter would merely bring the former to "higher perfection."

The Christian view of the fall now had to be accommodated to this pagan conception of "nature" as well. The Scriptural view of a center of human nature in the heart, the religious root, had been abandoned in favor of the Aristotelian concept viewing "reason" as the origin of human nature. Thus it could no longer be admitted that human nature is depraved in its very root because of the falling away of the heart from God. Instead, it was taught that "nature" was not completely spoiled by sin, but merely "wounded," that is, the supra-natural gift of grace had been lost.

### Aristotle: the pagan idea of the state. The state as the highest bond of human society, of which all other societal relationships are but dependent parts

What did this mean in terms of the idea of the state? The state was counted with the so-called "natural realm" and the pagan, Aristotelian view was taken over. This view came down to this: The state is the highest form of the community. All other societal relationships, such as marriage, family, blood relation, vocational and industrial groupings, all these are merely lower components which serve the higher. According to Aristotle, the state is grounded in the "rational-moral" nature of humankind. One cannot realize one's natural perfection in isolation, but only within the community. Nurture of marriage and family are the first, "lower" necessities of life, the "next higher" are fulfilled by the village community. But these lower societal relationships are not autonomous; only the state can, as perfectly autonomous community, provide a person with all that which serves the perfection of that person's "rational-moral" nature.

Thus the relation between the state and other temporal societal relationships is constructed according to the scheme of *the whole and its parts* and of the *goal and the means,* from the *"lower" to the "higher."* The "lower" relationships as different kinds of parts of the state have no goal in themselves, but all must serve the state. By nature the human being is state-oriented, for already in the forming of marriage, family, and blood-relations the natural compulsion to form the state is germinating. By nature the state precedes the individual. The state is implicit in the rational-moral nature, as the mature form of a plant in its seed, or the full-grown body of an animal in its embryo.

POLITICAL PHILOSOPHY

### The pagan totalitarian idea of the state and its revival in National-Socialism and Fascism

This Aristotelian idea of the state was the philosophical expression of the ancient Greek popular conviction. People really saw the state as the highest rung of humankind's moral development, as the highest and most perfect body to which the free citizen had to subject all areas of life. It was very much like the idea of the totalitarian state as recently taken up by Fascism and National-Socialism, although there the idea is no longer based on a so-called "metaphysical" order of reason, but is oriented irrationally to the community feeling of the people (*das Volk*).

Originally this pagan view of the state was grounded in the doctrine that human existence is rooted in a "rational moral" nature, that from this spring the directions of life, and that reason is the supra-temporal center, the deeper unity of human existence. As we have seen, this view is directly opposed to God's Word-revelation in Jesus Christ. It originated from an idolatrous, apostate conception concerning the center of a person's being, from a lack of self-knowledge caused by an idolatrous conception of God (making "reason" divine).

### The truly Christian view of the state takes its stance in the supra-temporal root-community of redeemed humanity in Christ Jesus

Christian religion had laid the axe to the religious root of this pagan idea of the state, and with that to the root of the whole pagan conception of temporal society. It revealed the true supra-temporal root of all temporal human societal structures grounded in the God-created world-order, that is, the religious root-community of humankind in the kingdom of God, which must reign in the heart of a person.

That deepest root-unity of humankind had fallen to the kingdom of Satan through Adam, but through Christ it has been redeemed and renewed.

Thus the "Church of Christ" – not in temporal diffused form, but in the supra-temporal unity in Christ – is the true root of all temporal societal relationships as required by God in His creation plan, just as all the temporal functions of human existence – physical movement, biotic life, feeling, thought, justice, morality and faith – must stem from the heart, the religious center.[1]

### All temporal societal relationships ought to be manifestations of the supra-temporal, invisible church of Christ

In other words, all temporal societal relationships, including state and organized church-institute, are, in accordance with their God-willed structure, merely temporal manifestations, temporal expressions of the one and only

---

1 *Editorial note* (DFMS): Dooyeweerd *first* realized that the human selfhood transcends the diversity of modal aspects and individuality-structures and *then* developed his philosophy of time in which he restricts time to the modal aspects and the dimension of individuality-structures. Consequently, since the human selfhood was considered to be supra-modal and supra-structural, the central religious dimension to which it belongs was considered to be supra-temporal.

true supra-temporal root-community of renewed humankind in the "body of Christ," the "invisible church" of which Christ is the only Head.

## The kingdom of God as the all-embracing rule of God

We see here that Christianity proclaims a total rule of God, opposed to the pagan idea of the total state as light is opposed to darkness. Paganism, unable to transcend time, seeks a last and highest temporal bond of which all other societal relationships can be no more than dependent parts. Christianity does not place a temporal church-institute above the state as an ultimate bond, but in Christ it looks beyond time toward the total theocracy, the invisible church of Christ. Here all temporal societal relationships are rooted and grounded, and each of these, after its own divine structure and God-given law, must be an expression, be it an imperfect one, of that invisible kingdom of God.

This basic Christian idea[1] of the kingdom of God is the only possible ground for the Christian idea of the state.

## The Christian idea[2] of sphere-sovereignty over against the pagan view that the state is related to the other societal structures as the whole to its parts

This idea of the kingdom of God is directly opposed to the apostate view of temporal society, that is, the self-willed, rational view which construes the mutual relation and deeper unity of temporal societal bonds as one of part and whole; one total state and the other societal relationships its parts. But neither marriage, nor family, nor blood-relation, nor the free types of social existence, whether they are organized or not, can be considered as part of an all-embracing state. Every societal relationship has received from God its own structure and law of life, sovereign in its own sphere.

The Christian world- and life-view, illumined by the revealed Word of God, posits sphere-sovereignty of the temporal life-spheres over against the pagan totality-idea.

However, if this idea of sphere-sovereignty is typified as peculiarly Calvinistic, we must protest. We must protest also when other views, which reject this sphere-sovereignty because they themselves have compromised with pagan philosophy, are considered as at least comparable Christian views. There is only *one* Christian view concerning human relationships which indeed takes seriously, without compromise, the Scriptural principle[3] of the kingdom of God.

---

1 *Translator's note*: Dutch *grondgedachte* (I shall occasionally note the Dutch for this word and similar ones.)
2 *Translator's note*: Dutch: *idee*.
3 *Translator's note*: Dutch: *grondgedachte*.

### The Roman Catholic view of the Christian state – Thomas Aquinas – is a falling away from the Scriptural conception

Roman Catholic thought concerning human society fell away from this Scriptural basis when it compromised with Aristotelian philosophy. It accepts the Aristotelian idea of the state for the area of "nature" and believes it can accommodate this to the Christian idea of the total rule of God by building another level, the realm of "grace," above the pagan edifice of nature.

But this departure from Scripture also penetrated views concerning the grace of the "Civitas Dei."

### Infiltration of the pagan totality-idea in the Roman Catholic concept of the church

It was not foreseen that the pagan totality-idea, which seeks in temporal society an "ultimate bond" of which all else can only be parts, would influence the Roman Catholic *view of the church*.

The state was seen in pagan manner as the totality of all temporal societal relationships in the *natural* (rational-moral) area. Now in turn it is looked upon as a lower serving part of the temporal church-institute. The church was now considered to be the total bond of all Christendom, the rule of the realm of grace in its temporal manifestation. In other words, the temporal church-institute with its papal hierarchy came to be identified with the so-called "invisible church," the supra-temporal kingdom of God in the body of Christ.

### A false view of the Christian state: the state is subject to the temporal church-institute

This immediately had a fateful influence upon Thomas' idea of the Christian state. Its Christian character was not Scripturally sought in the expression of Christ's Kingdom within the inner structure of the state itself. Rather, Roman Catholicism continued to see the inner structure of the state in the old pagan way as the total bond of all natural society, and continued to deduce the principles for political life by "natural reason," detached from revelation.

The state can participate in the realm of grace, not from within but, since it is itself strictly natural, can do this only by enlisting in the service of the temporal church-institute. This service consists of the eradication of heresy and paganism, and the subjection of the state to church leadership in all things that the church judges to touch the welfare of souls. In that view such and only such a state can be called Christian.

### Penetration of this view in modern denominational political parties

This Roman Catholic error continues even today in all those semi-Christian political conceptions that consider the Christian character of the state to consist of its ties to a given church-institute (thus in general every denominational grouping in politics).[1]

---

1 *Translator's note*: Dooyeweerd mentions some Dutch political parties in this connection, which are omitted here.

The notion that the Christian state must recognize a certain denomination as "state-church," or at least as the only true church, or that the Christian state must bend to a certain creed, as being the "only true one," the status of official legal authority, essentially stems from this old conception of Roman-Scholasticism which ascribes the totality of all temporal revelation of the body of Christ to just such a temporal church-institute.

### The Reformation over against the Roman Catholic view of Christian society

From the very start the Reformation has protested vehemently against this basic error. For its starting-point it returned to the invisible church, the supra-temporal body of Christ. It placed itself squarely over against the Roman Catholic *identification* of this invisible church (the total rule of God) with the temporal church-institute. The Reformation broke with the Roman Catholic view concerning the relation of nature and grace, at least theologically. It rejected the Church's teaching that the fall has not corrupted the root of 'natural existence', but has only caused a "supra-temporal gift of grace" to be lost. Consequently, the Reformation condemned the Roman Catholic doctrine of "natural merit of good works" and proclaimed again with power the good message of justification by faith alone.

And yet, this Scriptural, radically Christian foundation did not, especially in Luther, consistently penetrate the Reformation's view of temporal human society and its conception of the Christian state.

### Nominalism in Late-Scholasticism

Already in the late Middle Ages (14th century), a line of thought had turned itself in opposition to the compromise that Thomas Aquinas had sought to effect between Christian faith and Aristotelian philosophy. This line of thought was to become of world-wide importance, and is known by the name "Late-Scholastic Nominalism." The father of this movement was the English Franciscan William of Occam. What did this movement want? As we saw above, the whole Aristotelian-Thomist view of the "realm of nature" (as distinguished from the "realm of grace") was rooted in an absolutization of rational functions. In the Being of God intellect was also held to be predominant. This idea had come out most strongly in Thomas's thesis: The good is not good because God commands it, but God *had to* command the good, since it was good. That is, it was grounded in the general *concept* of good because it agrees with the "rational-moral" nature of a person. This was in flagrant disagreement with the Scriptural teaching of God's sovereign will. The Creator, far above all human measure, is not Himself subject to a law, for He is the Origin of all law, the Origin also of the norm of good and evil.

### The nominalistic conception of the law as subjective arbitrariness and the Thomistic idea of the law as rational order

The nominalist movement wished to reassert God's sovereignty as Creator over against Thomas's deification of reason in the realm of nature. But how did it go about this? Instead of positing truly Scriptural thought over against

POLITICAL PHILOSOPHY

Thomas it explained God's holy, sovereign Creator's will as despotic voluntarism. Nominalism spoke of *Deus exlex,* that is to say, a God whose laws are grounded purely upon disposition. God, Occam thought, could just as well have willed an egotistical moral law instead of the Ten Commandments.

Of course, Nominalism, distorting the Christian teaching of God as sovereign Creator into a tyrannical voluntarism divorced from the holiness of God, overthrew Thomism, which had championed a doctrine of a rational moral nature, and of a natural moral law grounded in reason. The law as general rule rooted in reason, loses, in this nominalism, the lofty position Thomas had accorded it in his rationalistic world of thought. The law is pulled down to a lower level. God Himself is not bound by law. But even Christians are elevated above the law, at least in their inner life of grace. Law is merely the positive ordering of temporal world-life, where sin reigns. And even when the Church and Scripture posit laws for external society, Christians have no longer anything to do with these ordinances in their inner life. They must subject themselves to this utterly incomprehensible positive command of the will of God, but only externally, and only as long as they move in the temporal world. From the inner life of grace the law has been removed.

**The nominalist dualism of nature and grace**

This nominalistic view of law radically destroyed the artificial compromise that Thomas Aquinas had attempted to construct between the pagan-Aristotelian conception of "nature" and the Christian understanding of "grace."

Thomas had taught: "nature" (understood in the rationalistic sense of Aristotle) is the lower, serving portal of "grace," the lower "matter" which, through divine grace of which the Church is the dispensary, is brought to "higher form" and higher perfection.

This line of thought became unacceptable to nominalism. "Nature" continued to be understood in all its manifestations in education, statesmanship, family life, etc. as the lower realm subject to law. But the natural order could no longer be considered as the portal to the order of grace. "Nature" as realm of law had come into implacable opposition to "grace" as area of Christian freedom (nominalistically understood). Now it was but one more step to identify the ordinances of "natural life" with the "sinful world," where harsh and inexorable law serves only to curb the wantonness of humankind.

There is really no place in such nominalistic thought for Christian learning, Christian political theory, or Christian organizational life. All of these belong in this view to the "kingdom of this world," to "sinful (human) nature," to the area of law, from which Christians have been freed in their inner life through grace in Christ. In no sense did created nature become any more Christian than it had in Thomas' thinking. On the contrary, it was completely cut off from the church, put on its own feet, and left to its own laws, as an autonomous area over against that of grace. Thus it was that nominalism, in bitter opposition to the hierarchical view of Thomas and his followers, began everywhere to resist the supremacy that the church-institute had exercised over education, economic life, etc. during the era of the 10th to the 13th centuries – "nature" and "grace" were separated, unbridgeably so.

### This dualism was perpetuated in Luther's law-gospel polarity

Luther had been brought up in this nominalistic line of thought before he made his appearance as Reformer. His own testimony is: "Ich bin von Ockham's Schule." Although Luther's life and mighty faith broke radically with Roman-Scholasticism in theology and church-life, and thus opened the way for the further development of the Reformation, he still retained in his world- and life-view the old nominalistic dualism of nature and grace, now as the polarity of *law* and evangelical *freedom*.

### Melanchthon's synthesis

Melanchthon[1] was soon able to search once more for a synthesis between Luther's reformational view of Scripture, classical philosophy, *and* the contemporary humanistic way of thinking which continued the nominalistic strain in the realm of nature and proclaimed human personality as sovereign ruler of the cosmos.

### Brunner continues Luther's dualism

In contemporary thought this dualism has been consistently carried through in Karl Barth and Emil Brunner. Hence their fundamental rejection of the idea of Christian culture, Christian learning, and Christian political life.

Brunner, in his *Das Gebot und die Ordnungen,* teaches the autonomy of the whole natural realm of ordinances (the area of law) over against the grace-realm of the Christian faith which is not subjected to the law (ordinances), but acts in freedom in accordance with the evangelical command of love. The latter does not posit a general rule for action, but is, according to Brunner, nothing other than the voice of a calling God who places us at every turn before the responsibility of a single, concrete decision, never to return in the same form. Christian love, in his view, never acts in accordance with principles. It is in the full sense of the word *unprincipled.* The Christian statesman, as politician, must never reach for the impossible ideal of a Christian political theory according to Christian principles. The command of love, says Brunner, heard in faith, certainly calls that statesman to political activity, but for the fulfillment of his task it points to the "natural ordinances," to political life with its "law unto itself" – a law which is in effect in contradiction with Christian love. The Christian need never rationalize this contradiction; the whole sinful world, according to Brunner, is full of it.

However, when certain existing laws do not allow Christians the freedom to fulfill their task of love toward their neighbors, then they must strive for a better ordinance, also politically. But here again, it is not faith that decides, but

---

[1] *Editorial note* (DFMS): Melanchthon initially supported Luther, subsequently showed sympathy with the Calvinistic doctrine of the Lord's supper and finally reverted to a more humanistic position which rejects the radical fall of humankind – reminiscent of the admiration he had in his youth for the great leaders of the humanistic movement: Agricola, Erasmus and Pirkheimer.

only natural reason, which the Christian has in common with all humankind. Therefore, no Christian political parties, but rather the greatest possible cooperation of all concerned, regardless of their life-view or their religion. According to Brunner, such a cooperative group can, in a realistic manner, work towards a given political improvement, for example in his case, to do away with today's mammon-inspired capitalist system. Christians may not always find the necessary support of the existing parties for their program. Or, perhaps these parties are possessed of such a demonic spirit that Christians cannot possibly become involved with them. If that is the case, Christians may decide to form a temporary group of their own, Brunner suggests, but at no time do they have the right to call such a party "Christian."

**Calvin breaks with the dualistic nature-grace scheme**

The truly radical break with the nature-grace scheme, inaugurated during the Middle Ages, really began with Calvin. With that radical break the way was finally and truly opened up toward building the Christian world- and life-view in the Scriptural sense, without compromise with paganistic and humanistic lines of thought.

In Calvin we no longer find law placed over against nominalistic evangelical *freedom*. Paul's message of the Christian's freedom from the curse of the law and his rejection of Pharisaic self-justification go hand in hand with the Scriptural view that each creature is subject to God's ordinances, completely and universally. An ordinance of creation is not to be viewed, as nominalism taught, as a divinely despotic command only valid for the lower area of "nature" and to be obeyed only externally, but as a holy, wise, and perfectly good ordinance of the Highest Majesty, without Whom the created cosmos would fall apart in utter chaos.

**Calvin's Scriptural view of law**

Thomas Aquinas, following Aristotle, taught that the temporal ordinances of God find their deeper unity in a rational idea of God. But for Calvin the deeper unity lies in the religious fulness of God's law: service toward God with the whole heart. Created human nature is, whenever Calvin allows Scripture to speak, no longer concentrated in the rational-moral functions, but in the heart, the supra-temporal religious root of human existence. Thus Scripture could be understood again. Christ, the New Root of reborn humanity, is the Fulfiller of the law, that is, He has fulfilled the law of God in the religious fulness and unity of its meaning.

This radically Christian beginning of Calvin's world- and life-view *had* to become of far-reaching significance for the whole Calvinistic conception of the relation between temporal cosmos and supra-temporal kingdom of God in Christ Jesus.

**The law as boundary between God and creature**

Calvin sees the law as the actual boundary between the sovereign God and His creature, and takes this law as divine ordinance in its deepest meaning to be *directed to the heart* as center, not to "reason." Only God is not subject to this law, not because His will would be despotic, but because His holy, wise, and perfectly good will is the Origin of all norms for good and evil. God gave every temporal sphere of life its own law in accordance with His will.

## Calvin's view of the divine creation-order contrasted with Thomas Aquinas

Calvin chose his starting-point in the supra-temporal religious root-unity of the divine law as revealed by Christ Jesus and fulfilled by Him. Therefore, with respect to the temporal fulness and diversity of ordinances which God has laid down in temporal life, the insight had to follow that none of these temporal spheres can be derived from or valued lower than any other.

Aristotle and Thomas, as we saw earlier, did think that the spheres could indeed be derived and valued in that manner. But then their conception did not spring from the Scriptural view of the true supra-temporal root-unity and Origin of divine law, but from self-willed human rational constructs. It sprang from the autonomy of reason and considered the rational-moral functions the actual supra-temporal and "immortal" center of human existence. Thus, this view also claimed the divine world-order to be an order originating in reason, where all spheres of life are ordered in an ascending scale from lower to higher, from means to end. In the realm of natural society the state became the highest bond – all other relationships were considered its serving parts.

But from a truly Scripturally Christian standpoint such a view of the divine world-order, which is essentially pagan, cannot but be radically rejected. For only then do we begin with the true Root of creation, Christ Jesus as fulfillment of divine Word Revelation. From here the root, the supra-temporal unity, the deeper unity of all creation, is seen in Christ, Whose Kingdom has been established in people's hearts. From this standpoint the true Origin of all temporal ordinances is not seen deified in "reason," but in the holy will of God, the sovereign Creator.

## The principle[1] of sphere-sovereignty: Calvin and Althusius

From this truly supra-temporal Christian religious standpoint the relationship among the temporal ordinances can only be understood as sphere-sovereignty. This basic, cosmic principle Calvin grasped in essence, and worked out with great clarity in his teaching regarding the temporal church-institute maintaining its inner independence from the state.

In the 17th century a Calvinistic German jurist, Johannes Althusius, oriented his social teaching to this principle.[2]

## The greater influence of Melanchthon's synthesis predominates

But this Scriptural line of thought could not immediately develop unhindered. The predominant influence of Melanchthon's synthesis program – another

---

1 *Translator's note*: Sphere-sovereignty is often referred to as a *"grondprincipe"* = *basic principle*.

2 *Translator's note*: Cf. *The Politics of Johannes Althusius*, Abridged and translated by Frederick S. Catney, with a Preface by Carl J. Friedrich, Boston: Beacon Press, 1964.

compromise between Christian and pagan thought – held sway in Protestant universities and from there took over leadership in practical life, particularly in political life. Calvin had not been able to free himself completely from Greco-Roman political theory, but Melanchthon once again sought his footing there!

Under these circumstances the Christian idea of the state relapsed into medieval Scholastic patterns: the state, part of the realm of "nature," could only receive its Christian stamp through serving the temporal church-community; except that, instead of a Roman Catholic church-institute, it was now the state-church. Again the basic motive of the Reformation was caught in an intrinsically impossible synthesis with pagan philosophy. No wonder that the ensuing ages have witnessed a gradual decline of the principles of the Reformation.

A new life- and world-view began to triumph in modern Western culture. Humanism, utterly oriented to this temporal life, placed sovereignty of the human personality at the center. Originally it had joined the Reformation, struggling to overthrow the rule of the church-institute over all natural life, but now it pushed its former ally into a corner.

### The rise of the modern humanistic world- and life-view

Humanism secularized the message of Christian freedom and of creation, fall, and redemption. Scripture's revelation of creation by God was gradually displaced by the idea of the creative power of science. Christian freedom was metamorphosed into sovereign freedom of the human personality. The humanistic world- and life-view was concentrated in two ground-motives: the humanistic ideal of personality and the new science-ideal. The first meant to teach absolute autonomy, self-sufficient "ethical determination." The second was intent upon a construction of the temporal world coherence, based on the "autonomy of scientific thought."

### The overpowering influence of the new mathematical science-ideal upon modern culture

Very quickly this new world- and life-view assumed a leading role in the shaping of modern culture. Leadership of science (*Wissenschaft*) was in humanistic hands. The new humanistic science-idea was inspired by a motive of dominance, a striving for power – the whole world was to be subjected to the sovereign human personality. Very quickly it oriented itself to the mathematical natural science which arose in the 16th century.

The new humanistic science-ideal received a dominant importance in the humanistic world-view and with its individualistic and rationalistic consequence it was simply impossible to combine it with a recognition of the Christian principle of sphere-sovereignty, because in the latter is posited a rich diversity of the temporal cosmos in inner indissoluble coherence of its differentiated aspects. Instead of God's sovereign will as Creator, creative mathematical thought was declared to be the origin of all laws that regulate temporal life. And since mathematical thought seeks to construct all complex figures from the simplest elements, humanistic philosophy tried to do the same with the complex whole (oneness) of the temporal world. Insofar as it was able to be consistent in its application of the new science-ideal, humanism tried to deduce all temporal order from one single, simple, natural-scientific law. Thus the British philosopher Thomas Hobbes (17th century) tried to construe the temporal cosmos theoretically from a mechanistic principle of attraction and repulsion.

The other pole, the humanistic personality-ideal with its idea of freedom did not become predominant in humanistic philosophy until later.

### The humanistic ideal of science continues in the modern individualistic idea of the state

When applied to temporal society, this new science-ideal led to the view that all societal relationships from family to state and church must be constructed from their "simplest mathematical components," here meaning individuals, abstract units. It was held that these individuals must be thought of as originally in a "state of nature" where perfect equality and freedom reigned. But now, in a so-called "social contract" they have given up more or less of this freedom to the state, the *body* of citizens.

It is obvious that this view was permeated with remnants of nominalism: positive ordinances that hold within the societal bonds were understood in terms of the arbitrary will of individuals united in a social contract. The constitution was then the *"volonté générale"* (general will). No individual can complain of injustice for in the social contract (Rousseau: *contrat social*) that person agreed to all laws the state might impose.

### Relativizing character of modern individualism in its view of society

This individualistic view of society, fruit of the new humanistic ideal of science, erased all the limits or borders that God in His wisdom had set in His temporal world-order. For every societal relationship (family, state, church, etc.) God has posited its own law of life; He created in each of them an inner structure, in its own sovereign sphere. But on the strength of its entire scheme humanistic rationalism had come in conflict with such a creed. All societal relationships were explained in terms of a uniform abstract scheme of social contract.

### Humanistic natural law over against its Aristotelian-Thomistic counterpart

The school of humanistic natural law (from Hugo Grotius to Rousseau, Kant and Fichte) defended this individualistic theory of society.

We are here dealing with a doctrine that differs in principle from that of the Aristotelian-Thomistic line. True, the latter also started with natural right, that is, the rational principles of justice and morality that are created part and parcel of human nature. But here an individual human being was not considered to be self-sufficient by nature, but was a member of the social community, the state. Aristotle and Thomas had taught that by nature the state preceded the individual. Thus they in principle rejected any individualistic conception of a natural state without societal relationships. They did not want to construct a state arising from the individual, like humanistic natural law, but rather the other way around – the individual from the state.

## Two mainstreams in humanistic natural law and the idea of the *Rechtsstaat* in its first phase of development[1]

We can distinguish two main streams in the development of humanistic natural law (1) *state-absolutism* (Grotius, Hobbes, Pufendorff, Rousseau, and others), where all freedom of the individual is lost to the state, and (2) *anti-state absolutism* (Locke, Kant, and others ), which starts from inviolate absolute constitutional rights of the individual over against the state, and thus seeks to limit the state task to organized safe-guarding of these rights.

From the latter came the *old-liberal theory of the Rechtsstaat* with its doctrine of the inviolate constitutional rights of the individual (such as freedom of the press, free enterprise, free association, etc.), and with its teaching of the separation of powers (separate legislative, executive and judicial powers). In practice, this theory has become a powerful co-influence in the modern idea of the state, but in its individualistic-humanistic basic conception it was in a sense Christian in origin. That basic conception underlies the old-liberal *"laissez faire"* program that rejects any "encroachment" of the state on economic life, particularly in industry.

## The old-liberal view of the *Rechtsstaat* and the separation of Church and State

That basic conception also underlies the humanistic idea of tolerance in the old-liberal sense, which seeks complete separation of church and state, and constructs the temporal church-institute as a private organization, again with the help of a uniform social contract – an organization where the individual is the sovereign authority (collegial or congregational type of church government). There is no room for a truly Christian idea of the state. The Christian religion has been relegated to the inner chamber.

## Tolerance in State-absolutism

In opposition to this main stream, however, the other movement in humanistic natural law, State-absolutism, taught the absolute sovereignty of state over church, and denied the church any internally independent law-sphere (this is so-called territorial church-government: the state has to maintain tolerance within the church; it opposes any doctrinal discipline). Such were the tenets of Hugo Grotius and the Arminians, and in Germany particularly Thomasius.

---

1 *Translator's note:* There is no English equivalent for the Dutch (and German) term *Rechtsstaat*. The term can be applied to a state in which a constitutional or accepted law and order is maintained, e.g. in sentences like: The *Magna Carta* safe-guarding the English *Rechtsstaat;* Hitler abolished the German *Rechtsstaat* and replaced it with his dictatorial National-Socialist *regime*. Elsewhere, Dooyeweerd also uses "rule of law."

The natural law idea of the state in Anti-state-absolutism with its own particular view of the *Rechtsstaat* has been linked unjustly with Calvinism. Liberalism (Otto Gierke in Germany, Eigeman in the Netherlands) was always intent on presenting the Calvinistic idea of sphere-sovereignty as derived from the liberal natural law view of the state. Even a Calvin scholar, the well-known Frenchman Doumergue, saw in Calvin the fore-runner of the ideas of freedom of the French Revolution. It is true that the Calvinistic idea of the state has been infiltrated at times with humanistic natural law; but, insofar as that is the case, it must be seen as nothing less than a falling away in principle from the Scriptural, Christian view of the state.

**The Calvinistic view of sphere-sovereignty has nothing in common with the humanistic freedom-idea of natural law**

After all, humanistic natural law begins with a supposed sovereignty of the human personality and that taken individualistically. Calvinism begins with God's sovereignty, revealed in religious fulness in the supra-temporal kingdom of Christ, and intended to shine forth from this root-community in all temporal societal forms. Humanistic natural law recognizes only "constitutional rights" of the individual, but it misjudges and levels the genuine societal structures as they have been embedded in the temporal world-order through God's sovereign will as Creator. That is why humanism, when it comes to the relation between state and other societal structures, can only base this relation on the natural (i.e., born-into) rights of the individual.

Again, Calvinism takes its starting-point from the Scriptural message of solidarity, from the religious root-community of humankind in creation, fall, and redemption. From this supra-temporal religious structural complex we behold the richly diversified panorama of temporal societal structures. In this God's sovereign will holds for all people. Therefore, these structures cannot be constructed after a scheme of a whole and its parts or a relativized individualistic social contract: they can be understood in their mutual relation only by way of the principle of sphere-sovereignty.

By the same token, whoever rejects this Scriptural principle *cannot* understand the idea of the Christian state in its truly Scriptural sense. For, as we saw, the genuine idea of the Christian state begins with the religious ground-idea of a supra-temporal Christian church, which reveals itself temporally in all societal structures equally. Denial of sphere-sovereignty is the immediate consequence whenever one chooses a starting-point for a world- and life-view in temporal reality. Such a starting-point within temporal reality has occasioned the absolutization of reason by some thinkers; others made too much of a certain temporal societal relationship – church or state; still others overestimated the abstract, mathematical component that the individual was held to be, and consequently constructed and relativized all societal structures after the uniform scheme of social contract.

### The truly Christian idea of the state cannot be separated from a recognition of sphere-sovereignty

Since it appears that the truly Christian idea of the state stands in indissoluble coherence with the recognition of sphere-sovereignty, this principle must first be investigated more closely. The more so since its true sense is often no longer understood, even in our own circles. It is for this reason that "sphere-sovereignty" is constantly identified with the political principle of *autonomy*. This shows clearly that relativizing ideas are infiltrating our Calvinistic view of the state.

### The radical difference between sphere-sovereignty and autonomy

The principle of autonomy makes sense only when speaking of the relation of a given whole to its parts. One can speak of municipal and provincial autonomy within the state.[1] Municipalities and provinces are indeed parts of the state and have no other structure. But family, state, church, school and industry differ radically in their respective structure. They can never be related to each other as parts to a whole. Hence, from a Christian point of view it is meaningless to speak of an autonomy of family, church, school and industry within the state. The inter-relation can only be sphere-sovereignty. In the final analysis autonomy, as relative independence of the parts within the whole, depends upon the requirements of the whole. Only the government can decide how far the limits of municipal and provincial autonomy can reach in terms of a well-functioning state. And the power, i.e. the jurisdiction, of autonomous parts can never be original or un-derived from the whole.

### Autonomy is proper only to parts of a whole; sphere-sovereignty does not allow for such a relation

It is quite different with sphere-sovereignty. It rests solely and completely upon the structures that are in place for the societal relationships and that are founded in the temporal world-order by God's sovereign will. Societal relationships whose structures are irreducible, such as family, state, church, etc., always have an *original* sphere of competence, in principle limited with respect to each other. The boundaries of sphere-sovereignty therefore can never be set one-sidedly by one party in a certain societal relationship such as a state or a church. These boundaries are placed in the divine world-order and do not depend on human arbitrariness. In the fullest sense they exist "by the grace of God."

What then are these structural principles by which temporal societal relationships are instrinsically differentiated and through which is given the divine guarantee for their sphere-sovereignty?

A proper answer to this question is a prerequisite for the right insight into the Christian idea of the state. For how can we gain this insight if we construe the

---
1 Compare the "autonomy of local churches" with that of a larger church organization.

state as totality of all societal relationships, or derived from the individual, mathematically conceived? How can we gain insight into the state if its inner, God-ordered law-structure is negated? The various structures of temporal society and their sphere-sovereignty can be viewed only from society's deeper root-community which is the kingdom of God in Christ Jesus' invisible church.

### Sphere-sovereignty and antithesis go hand in hand in Kuyper

Dr. A. Kuyper (1837-1920), called by God to lead the Calvinistic *Reveil* after Groen Van Prinsterer's death (1876), repeatedly emphasized the laws that apply to the life of societal relationships. In spite of liberalistic scorn he persistently posited an antithesis against the deadening synthesis of his time, and recognized sphere-sovereignty as fundamental cosmic principle. This connection between antithesis and sphere-sovereignty was not by chance. It is exactly the search for synthesis of scriptural and pagan or humanistic views of society that muddles the insight into the law-structure of societal relationships and sphere-sovereignty. Synthesis caused this in the past and causes it today.

### Kuyper broke with nature-grace and distinguished between church as institute and as organism

Kuyper, following Calvin, broke radically with the Scholastic and Lutheran nature-grace dualism. In his view of the relation between the kingdom of God and temporal societal relationships Scripture broke through powerfully, and caused him to see a distinction between the church as temporal institute and as organism. He saw that the Christian idea of the state could not be Scripturally understood as long as its Christian character was considered to have been proven if and when the boundaries between church and state are diluted. Hence his objection to article 36 of the Belgic Confession. The invisible, supra-temporal church of Christ is the center for him that must be revealed, not only in the temporal church-institute, but equally in all societal structures: in the Christian family, the Christian scientific community, etc. The church as an organism is the hypostasis (foundation), the revelation of the invisible, supra-temporal church in all societal structures equally.

This great conception opened the way for a truly Scripturally Christian view of society. In recent years it has been worked out further in deeper investigation of the various structural principles underlying the bonds of temporal society.[1]

---

[1] Cf. Dooyeweerd's *A New Critique of Theoretical Thought*, especially Vol.III.
[Editorial note (DFMS): As mentioned this work forms part of the A-Series of Dooyeweerd's Collected Works (volumes A1, A2, A3, and A4) – currently being published by The Edwin Mellen Press.]

### Elaboration of Kuyper's views the first meaning of sphere-sovereignty, the sovereign law-spheres

If insight into these structural principles is to be gained, it is first of all necessary to obtain insight into the rich diversity of aspects manifest in temporal reality. These aspects become clearest to us when we compare our theoretical and our non-theoretical, everyday experience of things. In daily life we view a blossoming apple tree as a complete unity, an individual thing. For the various sciences however, this one thing can be considered from a particular point of view or in terms of a certain aspect. For mathematics only the aspects of numerality and space; for physics only the aspect of motion; for biology, organic life; for psychology only under the aspect of being a sense-object; for logic as objective coherence of logical characteristics that we subjectively combine in the concept of a tree; for historians only as an object of human culture; for linguistics as receiving a name; for economics as object of appraisal; sociology considers the tree as object in human social functioning; aesthetically a tree is considered as an object of artistic harmony; jurally as an object of right of ownership, etc.; ethically as an object of love or hate; and theologically as an object of faith. (We believe that the tree is created by God and is not a fortuitous product of blind forces of nature.)

### Temporal aspects of reality in distinct law-spheres

Temporal reality functions in all of these aspects: in number, space, motion, organic life, feeling, logical analysis, historical form-giving, symbolic meaning (language), social manners, economic value, artistic harmony, justice, love, and faith. Furthermore, the full reality of a thing does not allow itself to be enclosed in any one of these aspects. For example, when a person says, in conformity with a materialist stance, that a tree is no more than a mass of moving matter, that person speaks nonsense since, by saying so, such a person forms a sense-perception and a logical concept of this thing, and gives it symbolic meaning in words. Implicitly therefore, that person recognizes that the numerical, spatial, and physical aspects are only certain sides of the real tree, and that these cannot be experienced without psychical feeling, logical understanding or language. These aspects of temporal reality cannot be reduced to each other either. Each has its own law-sphere, and is embraced in that law-sphere. Here the fundamental principle of sphere-sovereignty reveals itself in its primary sense.

### The religious root-unity of the law-spheres

The deeper unity of all temporal reality aspects within their own spheres of divine ordinances (law-spheres) cannot be found in any one of these aspects themselves. It is of a supra-temporal, religious character. The fulness of number, the spatial omnipresence, the fulness of force, of life, of feeling, of knowledge, of historical power, of communion, of beauty, of justice, of love, and of faith is in Christ Jesus, the Root of the reborn cosmos! In Him all these aspects of temporal reality find their true fulfillment of meaning, their deeper root-unity in the concentration upon service of God with the whole heart.

**As sunlight diffuses itself in prismatic beauty . . .**

As sunlight breaks into a marvelous diversity of rainbow hues, and as all these pure pastel colors find union in unbroken, shimmering white, so also do all temporal reality aspects find their supra-temporal unity in Christ Jesus, in Whom God has given us everything. All temporal aspects of created reality are in Christ Jesus, the true Root of creation, concentrated into the religious supra-temporal fulness of meaning. That is why, as Kuyper says, there is indeed no area of this life of which Christ does not say: Mine! There is no autonomous area of "nature" existing independently of Christ, above which His kingdom, a supposed "area of grace," looms as a superstructure.

**Common grace and the grace of rebirth** (*palingenesis*)**: no dualistic doctrine**

Nor is there a "realm of common grace" independent from a "realm" of "special grace" in Christ Jesus. The fall turned the heart, the root of creation, away from God. Creation therefore had to be reborn in its root through Christ. Special or saving grace can accordingly not be a "separate realm." It touches, as did the fall, the supra-temporal core, the heart, the root of all temporal creation. "Common grace" does not touch this supra-temporal root, but only the temporal ordinances of life: God halts the decomposition caused by sin. But this common, merely temporal grace of God has no other root than Christ Jesus. The grace of rebirth, given to us by God in Him, is the true hidden root of common grace which must be made evident in the "church as organism," that is, in Christian unfolding of life within all temporal structures of reality. When, by God's common grace in this sinful temporal life, culture, learning, art, family and political life, etc., are still possible, the inescapable call comes to the Christian to make Christ, as true Root of creation and as King of all temporal life, visibly manifest. For the Christian this task makes political life also a sacred Christian calling. It is true that under the rule of common grace Christ's kingdom cannot come to unbroken realization, for the power of sin continues to turn itself against this kingdom until the last day, but fundamentally in the root of Creation the victory has been won by the Lamb of God, and creation, in all its structures, has been maintained, saved, redeemed!

**Sphere-universality of the law-spheres**

If we find in all temporal aspects of our cosmos, as they are enclosed in their sovereign law-spheres, their supra-temporal unity and religious fulfillment of meaning in Christ Jesus, then this deeper unity must come to expression in each of these law-spheres. The theory of the law-spheres has indeed shown that every aspect of temporal reality expresses itself in coherence with every other. This phenomenon is called sphere-universality, the complement of sphere-sovereignty.

Here too, the analogy of the prism holds true, for in the seven colors of the spectrum every color is such that all others are mirrored in its particular tone. And as these seven colors are not indiscriminately mixed, but follow one another in a set order of wave lengths so also do the various aspects of temporal reality. They exhibit a set order of succession, from earlier to later.

## Succession of the law-spheres and the organic character of sphere-sovereignty

It can be shown that in the temporal world-order number precedes the aspect of spatiality. The latter in turn precedes motion, then, respectively, organic life, feeling, logical thought, historical development, language, economy, art and justice while, finally, the aspect for love precedes that of faith. No single aspect of reality and thus no single sphere of temporal divine ordinances can be considered as being independent from the others or purely by itself. Here the deeper unity of the law of God comes to rich expression. Whoever violates God's law in one temporal law-sphere does in reality violate the entire coherence of divine ordinances and in a deeper sense the religious root-unity of divine law as revealed to us through Jesus Christ. God's law is so rich and deep that in none of its temporal spheres does it permit only partial fulfillment. God's juridical ordinances cannot be repudiated without violating at the same time the norms for love, harmony, etc. The temporal world-order is a radically organic coherence even while it maintains sphere-sovereignty of the individual law-spheres.

This coherence is already guaranteed in the sphere-universality of which we spoke earlier. Let us take as example the aspect of feeling, investigated by the science of psychology. In this aspect, first of all, the bond with the aspects of number, space, and motion, which precede feeling in the temporal world-order, is maintained.

Furthermore, this bond with spatiality is mirrored in a sense of spaciousness and a sensory space-screen; in emotion we see the bond of feeling with the physical motion aspect of reality; in the sensuous or the sensory aspect the bond with the organs of a living body. This connection with the earlier, preceding aspects of reality can be shown not only in human life, but also in animal life.

In an animal, however, this life of feeling is limited to sensory feeling, tied to number, space, motion, and biotic organism. Human sense-life, on the other hand, displays a deepening and disclosure as compared to animal life, since here the psychical aspect reveals itself as connected also with the subsequent aspects of reality. A person also has a logical, historical, lingual, economic, and esthetic sense, a jural and moral sense, and a feeling of faith. Thus the meaning of number is disclosed and deepened in its coherence with the spatial and physical aspects of reality. And sense-life bound rigidly to the psychical, when opened up to the mental feeling of logic, justice, beauty, etc., is always directed by these later aspects upon which the disclosed psychical life anticipates.

## Disclosure and deepening of the meaning of a law-sphere

What we found with respect to feeling in temporal reality actually holds for all aspects of that reality in its order of sovereign spheres. Logical thought deepens itself from being strictly bound to sense-perception to theoretical, scientific thinking. Such opening up reveals a logical harmony of system, etc., in anticipation of the historical, the lingual, the economic and the aesthetic aspects of reality. So also the meaning of retribution of the juridical aspect opens up in anticipation of the ethical. One need only compare primitive retribution, where punishment was measured in terms of external result, with the modern retribution where, under influence of Christianity, punishment is determined in accordance with the measure of guilt and responsibility!

## The second meaning of sphere-sovereignty: individuality-structures in things and in societal relationships

The preceding brief summary of the main points of the theory of law-spheres, where the principles of sphere-sovereignty and sphere-universality are investigated, was necessary for an insight into the structural principles of the temporal societal relationships, such as the state, church, etc., in which the second meaning of sphere-sovereignty reveals itself.

In the normal experience of everyday life we never take hold of these aspects of reality in an articulated way; we do not distinguish them theoretically. Rather, these aspects are experienced implicitly in concrete things, events, relationships etc. Only science distinguishes and analyzes these law-spheres. But concrete things, events, and societal forms, immediately experienced, are based upon concrete, divine structural principles, in which the various aspects of reality are grouped in their individual way. Every concrete thing, be it a tree, a horse, a table, or a chair, functions in all aspects of reality. However, when we look more closely at the peculiar structural law of these things it becomes apparent that the various aspects are grouped in a different way in each of these structures.

## Concrete things function in all law-spheres indiscriminately. The significance of the typical qualifying function

For example, a tree undoubtedly functions in the aspects (law-spheres) of number, space and motion; in the first law sphere as a unity of the plurality of its roots, trunk, branches, leaves, etc.; in the second as a certain spatial figure; in the third as a moving mass of matter. But as long as we merely look at these aspects of a tree it is as yet senseless to speak of a tree. Mathematics, physics and chemistry do indeed eliminate the individual thing and investigate only the external relations in number, space, or motion. For them the peculiar inner structure of the thing functioning in them is not important. The physical law of gravity is valid for a tree just as it holds for a falling stone or planetary motion in the universe.

But when we shift our attention to the aspect of organic life things appear in a different light. For biologists, who study this reality-aspect, it makes eminent sense to speak of a tree. The organic life function, therefore, must take a very special place in the structure of a tree. This is the last aspect of reality in which the tree still functions as subject. In all later reality aspects it functions only objectively, as object. The tree lives as subject, but cannot sense psychically, can only be sensed as object. The tree does not think subjectively, but can be grasped as object in a concept. It is not a jural subject, but only an object of legal possession, etc.

However, the organic function has yet another role in the inner structure of the tree. For in this inner structure all the functions of the tree in earlier aspects of reality are typically directed toward their goal. Undoubtedly, the tree is subject to the general laws of mathematics and physics in its aspects of number, space, and motion. But in the inner structure of this thing, its functions in the three preceding law-spheres typically disclose and point to the destination of existence of the individual thing. In this inner structure no motion is purposeless. Chemical catalytic motions are typically pointed to the goal of tree-life. They are individually directed by the organic life-function.

### The first meaning of sphere-sovereignty (law-spheres) is not voided in the individuality-structure of things. The thing as individual totality

Hence we name this last function the typical end function of a tree, which finally qualifies the thing as a tree. Sphere-sovereignty of the various aspects has not been superseded with this. In the inner structure of the tree also, spatial relations do not become motions, nor do they become organic life processes. Thus the laws proper to these aspects of reality are not broken. But within this framework of sovereign aspects, the individuality-structure of the tree becomes apparent as individual whole. Here the various aspects are grouped in such a way that the organic life function has the role of guiding or qualifying function.

The structural principle, the inner structural law, cannot, therefore, be placed on equal footing with the divine laws of a given law-sphere such as number or space. It is rather a divine ordinance that overarches the distinct aspects of reality, and groups the individual totality of a thing in a particular way, in such a manner that a certain aspect, in this case the biotic, receives the role of leading function.

### The basic error of humanistic science: the attempt to dissolve the individuality-structure of a thing in a pattern of lawful relations within one aspect of reality

The primary error made by humanistic science (*Wissenschaft*) was the belief that the structural principle of things could be resolved in the laws of a single law-sphere. Thus it was thought that a living tree could analytically be construed completely as a complex of mechanical, material motion. The individual thing was theoretically resolved within one of its aspects (here mechanical motion), and the actual structural principle was left out of consideration.

Now, not only do the things of nature, such as a tree, or a mountain, or an animal, have their divine structural principles, but things formed by human skill (technics) have them too. In actuality temporal reality never exists without such individuality-structures. This in turn also holds for the various forms of society.

## The individuality-structure of societal relationships

Societal bonds such as family, church, school, state, etc., are therefore also individual totalities with their own inner structure. They too, cannot be reduced to or resolved into a single aspect of reality e.g., the economic or the juridical; in principle they function in all aspects of reality. They are radically distinguished from each other, however, in their inner structural principle for this determines the typical end function of a societal bond. This qualifying function gives the typical direction to all the functions of a societal structure in the prior aspects. It gives this structure its distinctive stamp, its particular qualification.

Thus an industrial unit is typically qualified as economic, that is, it has an inner structural principle whereby the various aspects of its reality are grouped in such a way that the economic aspect typically leads and directs all earlier functions. So also with the temporal church-institute: it is qualified as Christian community of faith based upon a common creed. That is to say, the inner structural principle of the church points to the faith-function as the typical qualifying function of this relationship, which typically leads and directs all earlier functions. Likewise the family: on the strength of its divine structural principle it is qualified as a typically ethical community of love between parents and children. And finally, the state is, in accordance with its inner structural principle, a societal relationship where the role of the qualifying function is fulfilled by the typically juridical community of rulers and subjects.

## The typical founding function

But the qualifying function alone does not yet determine the inner structure of societal relationships. In all these relationships this qualifying function points back to another aspect of reality, wherein the entire structure of a given relationship is typically based or founded. Consider the qualifying function of the family: the typical (ethical) parent-children love community. It is immediately clear that the expression of love between parents and children finds its actual basis in the natural blood-ties, in the natural genetic relationship. Now, this genetic relationship has its temporal foundation in the aspect of organic life, the biotic aspect of reality. And the typical community of love that has the role of qualifying function is thus founded in this biotic, genetic relationship – the natural blood-ties. This communion of love is not the same as the comradeship that one might expect in a labor-community. It is not the same as general neighborly love, or love among compatriots. Rather, it has its own unique structure based upon a genetic relationship.

The distinctive structure of the family relationship then is determined by the indissoluble coherence of (1) the ethical end function (the communion of love between parents and children) and (2) the biotic function of the genetic or blood-ties on which it is founded. This latter one we will call the founding function of this societal relationship.

In this way all societal relationships have their own qualifying function and their own founding function, both determined as such by the inner structural principle.

### The structural principle of the state. The state an institution required because of sin. This Scriptural view not maintained by Thomas Aquinas

What then is the structural principle of the state? The state as societal relationship is not like the family, founded in natural blood-ties. Rather its typical founding function is given in the historical aspect of reality – in a historical power formation, the monopolistic organization of the power of the sword over a given territory. Wherever this foundation is lacking we cannot speak of a state.

This typical founding function of the state reveals immediately that it is a divine institution required because of sin. Thomas Aquinas, and Roman Catholic political theory following him taught that the state as such is not instituted or required because of sin. Only the power of the sword is. The state is grounded in the nature of the human being and is the totality-bond of natural society. In other words, the power of the sword is, in the Roman Catholic view, not an essential part of the structure of the state. This is a falling away from the Scriptural view of the state as still strongly defended by the church-fathers, notably Augustine. This falling away is explicable in terms of the synthesis mentioned earlier – a synthesis of Christian doctrine and pagan Aristotelian theory. For, as we saw, the latter taught that the state is grounded in the "rational-moral nature," and as such is the total bond of which all "lower" relationships are never more than dependent parts.

### One-sided action for national disarmament is a neglect of the structural principle of the state

Whenever one denies the organization of the powers of the sword as typical founding function of the state's structure, one denies the structural principle proper to this societal relationship. It is then impossible to gain insight into the sphere-sovereignty of the societal structures. Thus it is clear that all action for one-sided national disarmament results from a denial of the divine structural law for the state. Anarchistic action against the state is then the (unwanted) outcome rooted in a misunderstanding of sin. The state is typically a divine institution of "common grace," i.e., the temporal, preserving (behoudende) grace of God. The power of the sword is not an end unto itself as modern imperialism teaches.

### The indissoluble coherence of the typical foundational function and the typical qualifying function of the state

In the divine structural principle of this societal relationship the power of the sword is unbreakably bound up with the typical qualifying function of the state, that is, the maintenance of a public jural community of rulers and subjects. All the intrinsic matters of state ought to be directed by this juridical nucleus, on the strength of the inner structural law. A state where the power of the sword becomes an end in itself degenerates into an organized band of highwaymen, as Augustine and Calvin have remarked.

A public community of law which, as qualifying function, qualifies the state, is utterly different from the internal jural community of other societal relationships, such as family, school, or church. In all of these the internal jural community is directed by the particular qualifying function of the relationship concerned. Internal church-order, for instance, coheres inseparably with the typical qualifying function of the temporal church bond as community of believers, united by a common creed, founded upon a historical organization of office. Think of church discipline, by which the purity of life and doctrine is maintained.

Only in the case of the state does the jural community itself operate as qualifying function, but always founded upon territorial organization of the power of the sword. The internal community of law of the state is a community of jural government, where the government, as servant of God, does not carry the sword inappropriately. The government may, in accordance with the state's inner law of life, never allow itself to be led by any other point of reference than that of justice. But there is no question of a private community of law, as in the other societal relationships, but a public one, subject to the jural principle of the common good. And precisely here, in the understanding of the principle of the common good, does the difference between Christian and pagan or humanistic ideas of the state become clearly evident.

### The "common good" (public welfare) as jural principle and as absolutistic principle of power

For, insofar as pagan or humanistic political theory is absolutistic, it views the principle of the common good from the idea that the state is the total bond of all temporal society. Of such a state then, all other societal relationships are no more than dependent parts. From this point of view it is impossible to see "common good" as a truly jural principle.

As long as the relation between state and other social structures is understood as a whole-parts relation, justice cannot prevail in the face of the "common good." And thus it is that out of necessity the state is granted, at least juridically, absolute jurisdiction and absolute competence. But absolute competence of authority cannot exist side by side with the very meaning of justice, for justice demands a balanced delimitation and harmonizing of jurisdiction. Yet, when the state is given absolute competence, it is assumed that the state as the wellspring of positive justice is itself above the law. Thus the teaching of the well-known sixteenth century Frenchman Jean Bodin: *Princeps legibus solutus est* – the government stands above legislated law.

The modern message of the citizen without rights in relation to the state as proclaimed by National-Socialism and Fascism, is but a consequence of such thought.

### The old-liberal idea of the *Rechtsstaat* proves powerless to control the absolutism of "common good"

The liberal idea of the *Rechtsstaat* proved inadequate and powerless over against the absolutism of common good. In its classical, individualistic dress of natural law it attempted to control absolutization by means of external restriction of the task of the state. The social contract that had supposedly inaugurated the state was intended to give the state no other task than the organized safe-guarding of natural, constitutional rights of the individual – life, property, and freedom.

### The humanistic idea of the *Rechtsstaat* in its second, formalistic phase

However, when historical developments confronted the state with a far broader task, and forced it to become involved with social and economic life, in culture, education, etc., this old-liberal idea too, became obsolete. Hence, it was now modified; the state is no longer limited in its task only to the protection of the rights of the individual. Many other "goals" may be striven for: furthering of culture, stimulation of economy, etc. But, the idea was that the state may only do this when remaining formally subject to administrative legislation. This new and fundamentally modified conception gave the citizen only formal protection against the absolutism of the so-called "common good." For after all, this protection lay only in the provision that the "executive" was formally subject to the law. But the law-giver as such was not curbed in any way by this formal idea of the *Rechtsstaat*. The juridical sovereignty of the law-giver was accepted unreservedly. With that the latter was placed above and beyond the law. Only the executive branch of government was subordinated to the legislative power.

### Only the Christian idea of the state, rooted in the principle of sphere-sovereignty, is the true idea of the *Rechtsstaat*

The radically Christian idea of the state, the idea that has fundamentally broken with any absolutization of either state or individual, is the proper idea of the *Rechtsstaat*. It alone can grasp the principle of the common good as a truly jural principle of public law, because it is grounded in the confession of a supra-temporal root-community of humanity in the kingdom of Christ Jesus, and because it accepts therefore the principle of sphere-sovereignty for the temporal societal bonds.

But to see the principle of sphere-sovereignty in the correct light, we must remember that it does not impose external boundaries on the task of the state. The old-liberal idea of the *Rechtsstaat* did this with its demand that the government refrain completely from any involvement with social and economic life. However, we have seen that every societal relationship – and therefore also in the state – in principle functions in all aspects of reality (law-spheres). It was the basic error of humanistic thought concerning the *Rechtsstaat* in its old-liberal, individualistic form that it maintained that the state could be understood as an abstract community of law, or rather as a simple juridical social contract, and nothing more. But the truth is that the inner structural principle of the state ought to express itself in all aspects of temporal reality equally. For the state is not merely a community of law, but also a spatial community (the country and its boundaries), a community of life, of feeling, of thought, of historical cultural form, and of social and moral dimensions (think of patriotism). And the Christian idea of the state demands that the structure of the state expresses itself also in a Christian community of faith, embracing both governors and those governed.

## The task of the state cannot be limited externally by excluding the state from certain aspects of reality

But imposing limitations on the task of the state in all these areas of life is an intrinsic limitation, determined by the inner structural principle of the state. The internal economy of the state relationship cannot, as such, express itself like the structure of a private business. Neither can the internal social community within the state relationship (for instance, national festivities, public ceremony, etc.) take on the form of the social community of a clan, or a family, or an association.

The public justice of the state finds its boundaries in the internal private communities of law of the other societal relationships. Thus also, the Christian state as such can reveal itself in the area of faith only within the boundaries of its own inner structural principle, and may not assume the structure of a church-institute. For the state is not, like the temporal church community, qualified as a community of believers in Christ. That is to say, neither the state, nor any other non-ecclesiastical societal relationship has as its typical goal the area of faith and confession.

## The state, with its function as political faith-community, may not be subjected to an ecclesiastical creed

For that reason the state may not be tied to a certain ecclesiastical creed, as was long the rule. Nor may the demand be made that offices in the state be held by candidates of a certain denomination, or group of denominations (e.g., Protestant or Roman Catholic). A confession concerning the task of a Christian government, such as the old article 36 in the Belgic Confession, does not belong in an ecclesiastical creed. And in the same way the Christian state as community of faith should not tie itself to a confessional creed concerning the sacraments and the preaching of the Word. The creedal basis of the Christian state in its function as community of faith can only be the confession of God's sovereignty revealed in the reign of Jesus Christ, the Governor of all governments on earth. But this political creed entails for all of state-life the recognition of the truly Scriptural basis for political life. And the heart of it all remains the confession of God's sovereignty in Christ Jesus in which is included the recognition of sphere-sovereignty of the various societal relationships.

## Christian faith deepens the typically political principles of justice. The Roman and the Christian idea of justice

These jural principles of the structure of the state, opened up and deepened by Christ's universally redemptive work, ought to take the leading role in the Christian state. Undoubtedly, in a pagan state God's common grace maintains the inner structural principle, but in that type of state political life in its faith-function is without its direction towards the kingdom of God in Christ Jesus. The true Root of common grace, Christ as supreme Governor, remains hidden in the pagan idea of the state – there is no visible manifestation.

For instance, classical Roman law, in spite of its admirable technical development, remained rigidly bound to an egotistical imperialistic idea of power and was without any disclosure and enrichment in the sense of a Christian idea of solidarity, in which power, love, and justice are caught up in the full sense of their religious root-unity, a unity majestically revealed to us in the cross of Christ.[1] Thus we find no trace of Christian social legislation in pagan Roman public law. The jural sphere of the pater familias (head of the Roman household), egotistically absolutized, is there in unrelenting opposition to the absolute imperialism of the Res Publica Romana. Over against this absolute imperialism the Roman citizen had no rights, for the state was thought of in a totalitarian sense as the whole of society. In private life, on the other hand, the egotistic spirit of Cain ruled: Am I my brother's keeper?

### The liberal-humanistic and the Fascist views of justice

In the modern humanistic view of justice one can rediscover this isolating Roman dualism of public and private law.

Old-liberal politics with its principle of exclusion raised private advantage to the highest directive of private life. And in the recent reaction against this liberalism by Fascism and National-Socialism it is true that great emphasis is placed upon common good and upon the requirements of the community of the people, also in the sphere of private law, but nevertheless, all this is at the cost of sphere-sovereignty and individual freedom. For here too, the old pagan idea of the state dominates an idea that teaches that the state is the totality-bond of which all others can only be dependent parts.

Only the radically Christian idea of sphere-sovereignty can keep the absolutism of "common good" in check. No other view allows us to see the true harmony among the various spheres of life, as willed by God in His creation-order. Hence it alone can reveal the truly Christian idea of the *Rechtsstaat*.

### All non-Christian theories of the state are essentially theories of power (Machtsstaatstheorieen)[2]

For the Christian idea of the *Rechtsstaat*, sphere-sovereignty is the cornerstone. In the final analysis all pagan and humanistic views of politics are in-

---

1  *Translator's note*: By "disclosure" (*ontsluiting*) and "enrichment" (*verdieping*) Dooyeweerd calls attention respectively to the unfolding expression of the retrocipatory moments, and the anticipatory moments, in this case within the jural sphere.

2  *Translator's note*: The term *Machtsstaat* is to be taken as the exact opposite of *Rechtsstaat*. In humanism, and already in Greek thought each represents a horn of the same (false) dilemma. Broadly, the idea of the *Machtsstaat* is a view of the state as characterized historically by power (the view of the sophist Kallikles, Machiavelli, Nietzsche, Hegel, etc.), while the idea of the *Rechtsstaat* views the state as characterized by natural justice, conceived apostatically as based on natural law, inborn right, absolute standards, etc. (Plato is a good example here.) In contemporary political theory these are in dialectical opposition to each other, and are often unsuccessfully forced together. This is what Dooyeweerd sees as the crisis in humanistic political theory. For a fuller explanation of this crucial point see *A New Critique of Theoretical Thought*, Vol.III, Part II, chapter 3, and *De Crisis in de Humanistische Staatsleer* (The Crisis in the Humanistic Theory of the State – N.V. Boekhandel H. TEN HAVE, Amsterdam, 1931, 209pp.).

variably theories of a *Machtsstaat*, because at best they can give arbitrary, but never true boundaries to the task of the state. It can be understood, therefore, that modern National-Socialistic and Fascist theories of the *Machtsstaat* deny the individualistic liberal idea the right to name itself with the proud title of idea of the *Rechtsstaat*.

### The true relation of state and church: not a mechanical division, but sphere-sovereignty

The radical difference between Christian and liberal humanistic political doctrine is nowhere clearer than in their respective views of the mutual relation between state and church.

Insofar as liberalism wished to safe-guard the freedom of church-life over against the state it could not do otherwise than (1) effect a watertight division between state and church, and (2) introduce the "religionless state," where faith is completely excluded. The freedom of the church was then derived from the absolute constitutional rights of the "religous individual." The church became a private association, and in it the "general will" of the members was declared sovereign.

Scriptural Christianity, on the other hand, can never take over this liberalistic slogan of separation of church and state without spiritual suicide. Sphere-sovereignty does not yield a watertight compartment or mechanical division among the areas of life. It is, as we have seen, an organically most deeply cohering principle, for it begins with the religious root-unity of the life-spheres.

### The inseparable, interwoven texture of the various structures of society

The various social structures by which sphere-sovereignty is internally guaranteed do not stand alongside each other in isolation. In temporal life they are intertwined and interwoven. All other societal relationships also have a function within the state, just as, conversely, the state functions in all other societal relationships. But in the final analysis all these structural interplays remain of an external character with respect to sphere-sovereignty. Members of a family, a congregation, or a business enterprise are at the same time citizens. And conversely, the state is always dealing with families, churches, and business enterprises. But the competence, the sphere of jurisdiction of the state can never be expanded into the internal, structurally determined concerns that are proper to these societal relationships without thereby violating in a revolutionary way the cosmic constitution of sphere-sovereignty. Chaos rather than order and harmony is then the inevitable result.

### The prophetic task of Christianity in these times

Thus the Christian idea of the state in its only possible, that is radical Scriptural, sense remains the liberating message – also, yes especially, in our volatile times. And it is to us, kindred in spirit, to take hold of this incomparably rich idea, to make it our own, to possess it spiritually as the heritage of our fathers. That we may carry it everywhere – for the benefit of the entire community, now so drastically tortured, as the only balm for its wounds.

# The relation of the individual and community from a legal philosophical perspective[1]

AN AGE OVERESTIMATING the individual is necessarily followed by one overestimating the community. This is also true of legal life and the philosophy of law.

Post-medieval legal philosophy, in its first period, is characterized by the modern humanistic doctrine of natural law as it was founded by Grotius. In reaction to this phase the second period emerged as the Historical School of Law and became the dominant trend in modern sociology.

**Individualistic and Universalistic conceptions of Law**

Theoretically seen, the individualistic doctrine of natural law is strongly influenced by the modern humanistic natural science-ideal. This ideal sets out to control reality by reducing complex phenomena to their simplest elements. Its aim is to analyze these elements with the aid of exact mathematical concepts in order to unveil the laws determining reality fully. The methods of mathematics and occasionally that of mathematical physics (Hobbes) serve as model in this regard. The modern doctrine of natural law similarly attempts to explain the organized communities of human society in terms of their elements, the individuals. It performs this jural construction on the basis of the social contract theory.

The Historical School and to some extent also the sociological doctrine of law are positioned against this individualistic and constructing approach in its advocacy of a universalistic view proceeding from the totality in order to understand its parts. This, however, is not done in a consistent way. The Historical School, for example, does not get beyond the people comprising the "totality of the national culture." From the individual folk nature of the latter, it asserts, the unique legal order, language, mores, art, etc. of that people flow as products of history.

With this the idea of an order of natural law itself, fitting all times and peoples, is rejected.

The struggle between these two main trends occupies a prominent place in the divergent evaluation of the Roman ius gentium (world law).

---

[1] This article appeared in the "Algemeen Nederlands Tijdschrift voor Wijsbegeerte en Psychologie," Year 39, Number 1, October 1946, pp.5-11 – under the title: *De verhouding van individu en gemeenschap rechtswijsgeerig bezien* (The relation of the individual and community from a legal philosophical perspective). *Translator*: D.F.M. Strauss; *Editor*: Alan M. Cameron.

The Germanistic wing of the Historical School viewed the reception of the *ius gentium* in Germanic countries of the continent as a forging of the "Germanic conception of law." The latter was supposed to be permeated to a great degree by a "social spirit." It viewed all law as displaying in principle the same character.

Roman law, by contrast, breathes the spirit of Cain, that of an unbridled individualism, and proceeds from a sharp separation between public law and private law. It causes the individual and the state to stand irreconcilably over against each other. The same concern is expressed in the dominant sociological doctrine of law. This approach still uses the (now outdated) depiction of the "spirit of Roman law" as a "spirit of disciplined egoism" in the way that it was put forward dramatically by von Jhering.

On the other hand, from its outset, the doctrine of natural law of the 17th and 18th century viewed the Roman *ius gentium* as the ratio scripta and as the residue of the true natural law.

One can follow this struggle in the divergent assessments of the modern codifications of civil law which, as an effect of the Enlightenment, were introduced in Prussia, France, Austria and presently also in The Netherlands.

The currently all-powerful historicistic and sociological views of law claim to recognize in these codifications the continual influence of the individualistic spirit of Roman law and a desire for a radical transformation of the "social spirit" which is, according to this view, already in the process of emerging. The call for a droit social as substitute for the droit individuel has become universal. Various national-socialistic jurists have already spoken about a "farewell to the Civil Code."

Within the idea of the droit social, seen as a communal demand permeating legal life in its entirety, an overestimation of the community-idea manifests itself, similar to the fashion in which the idea of a droit naturel managed to push the pendulum to the other extreme of an overestimation of individual freedom in the 18th century. For legal philosophy and for legal life the struggle between these two trends is a matter of serious concern.

If one looks at the humanistic doctrine of natural law only as an aprioristic construction, designed in a rigid way, as a legal system to fit all people and times and deduced by applying a mathematical method, then one views it too one-sidedly according to its theoretical and legal philosophic pretensions. For in this sense both its foundation and its method are no longer defensible.

But the doctrine of natural law also had a prominent practical tendency – something modern criticisms often have not recognized. This practical tendency is even present in the work of an author such as Grotius who had the intention of developing his doctrine of natural law fully independent of political issues, similar to the mathematician who constructs his figures entirely divorced from "matter."

## Civil Law and the idea of the State

Essentially this has initiated the quest of pursuing the basic principles of civil private law and the modern idea of the state. However, both these ideals were lost again during the medieval period since it came into conflict with indigenous Germanic legal practices that were still primitive in many ways. It also clashed with the feudal system, a whole complex of royal rights, privileges, and a diversity of property relationships reflecting differences in social rank (old farmer serfs, landlord serfs, church serfs and so on), all of which still strongly reflected the stamp of an undifferentiated society.

On the other hand, when the Roman world law was seen as ratio scripta and as a positive expression of natural law, then this view was fully consistent with the classical Roman jurists, for these latter maintained a close connection between the ius naturale and the *ius gentium* – so intimately that it sometimes was identified incorrectly.

The *ius gentium* was the first realization of a truly civil law within the Roman world imperium. It fundamentally differs from the older primitive ius civile, i.e. the Roman folk law. The latter can at best be compared with the primitive Germanic folk laws, as they were described in the leges barbarorum during the Frankian period.

This kind of folk law still belongs to an undifferentiated condition of society – a phase in which all law still displays only one character because as yet society did not know differentiated spheres such as that of the church, the state, commerce and business firms, free associational organizations, and so on.

Undifferentiated spheres of life, such as that of the familia, neighborhood, guilds (in the sense of brotherhoods or fraternities), the communal life of the Roman people and the tribe, still encompassed human life totally, with respect to all spheres of life. These spheres take on all tasks that, at a deepened level of cultural development, are performed by independent differentiated societal collectivities. The undifferentiated sphere of power of these collectivities, often strongly rooted in a pagan religion of life, is absolute and exclusive. The entire legal status of a human being, as a consequence, is completely dependent upon membership in these primitive collectivities. Whoever finds himself outside this bond is hostis, exlex, i.e. without any rights or peace. The undifferentiated community absorbs the individual according to that person's entire legal status.

This is also valid with regard to the old Roman familia where the head, the pater familias, had an undifferentiated power over all members, rooted religiously in the exclusive power of the house and hearth gods. This power was an absolute and exclusive dominium simultaneously incorporating authority and the competence to dispose of property rights. This undifferentiated concept of property was not close to an individualistic spirit at all, as was suggested by von Jhering. Much rather, it is an expression of the totalitarian primitive conception of community.

Civil private law is totally different from primitive folk law. It is the product of a long developmental process, giving birth to a differentiation of society.

As soon as the undifferentiated spheres of life are transcended, it becomes possible for the differentiated societal collectivities to manifest themselves. Then, according to their inner nature, no single one of them can any longer encompass the human being with respect to all spheres of life. Thus it becomes possible to acknowledge the rights of the individual human being as such, apart from all particular communal ties such as gender, race, nation, church orientation, social rank and status.

The human being as such now witnesses the allocation of an individual sphere of freedom that embodies the private autonomy of that person.

By virtue of its particular nature civil law does not accept a difference in principle between human beings on the basis of race, social status or rank – they all enjoy civil legal freedom and equality.

The classical Roman jurists understood this in terms of their idea of the *ius naturale*. This idea, because it is rooted in the intrinsic nature of civil law, brought to expression, in a pregnant way, the constant basic principles of civil law. In doing that, it sharply distinguishes itself from the Aristotelian idea of natural law which also comprises communal ties evincing inequality in position. These classical Roman jurists were justified in positing this essentially civil legal *ius naturale* as the basis of the Roman *ius gentium*. We have seen that they often even presented the two as being identical.

However, this identification is not valid, since the *ius gentium* continued to accept the institute of slavery and, therefore, in this respects deviated from the ius naturale. Furthermore, it only gave a completely historically determined positive form to the former.

The modern humanistic doctrine of natural law advocated this notion of the ius naturale to an increasing degree. During the Enlightenment it crystallized in the doctrine of innate and inalienable human rights.

Within modern differentiated legal life, civil law constitutes only one of the distinct spheres of private law. As such it is closely connected with the state.

The multiple spheres of private law are fully determined according to the differentiated structural principles of human society. For example, the sphere of internal ecclesiastical law, in its internal jural character and original sphere of competence, is delimited by the peculiar structural principle of the church-institute as institutional community of Christian believers within the organized service of the Word and the Sacraments. Ecclesiastical law unmistakenly evinces a private communal character and its own irreducible nature. It can never be delineated merely on the basis of its juridical genetic form (ecclesiastical rules of procedure), since within this genetic form ecclesiastical law may be interlaced with legal spheres of a different nature.

Similarly, there also exists the internal legal sphere of a modern factory, which, according to its internal character, is delimited by the structural principle of the firm as one that is qualified by the economic entrepreneurial organization of capital and labor.

This piece of private law, originating from the juridical form of the rules of procedure of the factory, also bears a specific communal character, though it lacks the typical institutional feature of ecclesiastical law since it completely rests on a voluntary basis.[1]

The same applies to the domain of law related to the sphere of interaction in trade and commerce. This domain is also economically qualified though it does not share a communal character. It exhibits a coordinational nature since individuals participating in this legal relationship are coordinated with each other and are not bound together into a durable unity.

We may consider in this regard the so-called "standard clauses" regularly incorporated in separate agreements reached within the different branches of trade and business. In spite of the fact that, as "generally accepted stipulations," they are acknowledged by civil law, these "standard clauses" have an internal nature different from civil law.

Each one of the different societal institutions has its own internal law (consider a social club, a philanthropic association, a trade organization, etc., etc.). All of them stand in service of, and are qualified by, the particular qualifying function of the societal spheres to which they belong. In that way they have a specifically organized communal character since the members of a corporation are organized into a unity.

Civil private law is not a specific law in this sense. In other words, it is not fit to serve, and qualified by, a typical internal guiding function which itself lies outside the jural aspect. It is a ius commune, a common law, as it is called by the British. By itself it has no other destination than to bring to expression the requirements of the ius naturale, of natural justice in the classical sense of the word,[2] as we have explained above.

According to its internal nature it is built upon the basis of individual human rights of freedom and equality. This character prevents it from having a communal nature. Therefore it has to be distinguished from the domain of what is known as social labor rights – a domain with its own unique constitution and destination.

The attempt to transform it into a communal law, according to the model of the modern idea of the droit social, inevitably cancels its civil legal nature. For the intrinsic nature of the different legal spheres is not something made by human beings, since, to every person forming law, it is a given, based upon the order and structure of reality.

Civil private law, in its nature, constitutes the juridical asylum of the human personality, the stronghold of individual freedom and as such it is destined to provide a beneficial counter balance against the excessive pressure of communal demands within legal life.

---

1 Translator's note: Dooyeweerd distinguishes between institutional and voluntary societal collectivities. Communities "destined to encompass their members to an intensive degree, continuously or at least for a considerable part of their life, and as such in a way independent of their will," are called institutional (A New Critique of Theoretical Thought, 1957, [NC] Vol.III:187).

2 *Editorial note* (AC): "Natural justice" in this context has to be distinguished from the same expression when it is applied in administrative law.

In our modern era, due to the reign of historicism and a naturalistic sociologism, this is hardly understood any longer. Both these spiritual trends are united in their historicistic view of human society, according to which everything is caught up in continual development and in a flowing transition. They do not have an eye for the constant structural principles that determine the nature of the different spheres of life and that themselves make all historical development possible in the first place.

The Historical School, in a dangerous fashion, starts to link civil law to the individual character and spirit of a people (Volksgeist) and in doing so it attempts to eliminate fundamental difference between civil law and primitive folk law. The attempt is accompanied by a serious attack on the classical Roman and the modern humanistic doctrine of the ius naturale. All forms of law are seen as the historical product of the peculiar disposition of a people (volk) which, therefore, in principle is communal law, bearing a typical "folk" character.

The Romanistic wing did not pursue the consequences entailed in this approach. It continued to adore the Roman world law in its classical phase of development as "ratio scripta," although it rejected the doctrine of the ius naturale.

But in the Germanistic wing the basic thesis of the Historical School initiated an assault against the "individualistic" *ius gentium* of the Romans. And modern sociology, disseminated from France, launched an attack against the "abstract metaphysics" of the ideas of freedom and equality.

It is remarkable that the attack against the foundations of civil law is always accompanied by an assault in principle on the modern idea of the state, which rests upon a sharp distinction of public and private law and on the principle of the salus publica in its clear separation from all group interest.

Leon Duguit, the French scholar in constitutional law, who required a "transformation du droit civil"[1] according to the spirit of a droit social, simultaneously proclaimed the statement l'état est mort.[2] But already in the case of Count St. Simon (with Auguste Comte the founder of positivistic sociology), we can see to what an extent the battle against the "metaphysical" doctrine of human rights is accompanied by an attack on the state, which, as the instrument of class domination, is destined to "die away."

We need not be surprised by this intimate connection in the fight against civil law and the state, since the internal law of the state, as ius publicum, shares with civil private law the absence of a qualification outside the jural guiding function. The state is, just as the church, an institutional community, though, through its structural principle, the state radically differs from the church. According to this structural principle the state is characterized as a public legal community of government and subjects on the basis of a monopolistic territorial organization of the power of the sword. The internal "destinational" function of the state is given in the creation of a public legal community, which

---

1 A "transformation of civil law."
2 "The state is dead."

stands in an indissoluble structural coherence with a typical historical foundation in a monopolistic organization of the power of the sword. The salus publica as fundamental principle of the public institutional law of the state essentially has to be conceived of as an idea of public law.

This presupposes in the first place that the state cannot assume an absolute sovereignty over the other societal spheres that differ in principle from the state.

Every form of legal power, that of the state also, is structurally delimited by the inner nature of the sphere of life within which it is exercised. For law finds its symbol in the scales of Themis. It requires, according to its nature, delimitation and counter-balance of every competence by another one.

As soon as one ascribes an absolute sovereignty to the state, one has abandoned the boundaries of law and collapses into state absolutism, based upon a deification of the state. Then also the idea of the salus publica degenerates into a lever for an unhampered state absolutism, echoing the frightening sound of the Leviathan, the "Behemoth."

The inner delimitation of the legal power of the state is given by the internal structural principle of this societal institution. The ius publicum, constitutive of the internal law of the state as public legal institution, does not permit service to group interests external to the jural qualifying function of the state.

Therefore, the nature of the state is irreconcilable with the allocation of privileges to specific persons or groups. Similarly, no individual or group may withdraw from the public legal power of the government within the sphere of life of the state.

## The State as Public Legal Institution

For that reason the state had to commence its entry into the world scene by starting to do away with the undifferentiated spheres of authority of private lords and societal collectivities which withdrew their subjects from the legal power of the state.

In order to achieve this aim the public legal principle of freedom and equality has to be pursued. It also forms the basis upon which civil legal private freedom and equality are to be attained. As long as it is possible for private lords and for private societal collectivities, to exercise an exclusive and undifferentiated power over their subjects, there is no room for a truly ius publicum and for a truly civil ius privatum.

It is only the state, on the basis of its public legal power, that can open up to the individual person a civil legal sphere of freedom, providing that person with a guarantee against the overexertion of power by specific private communities and also against an overexertion of the public legal power itself, as long as the public office bearers keep alive an awareness of the inner limits of their competence.

The state, in view of the inner nature of the ius publicum, does not have the competence to bind the exercise of civil private rights to a specific social-economic destination, simply because the ius publicum intrinsically lacks any specific economic qualification.

It lacks this competence also because civil law leaves it to private autonomy, in the exercise of civil private rights, to determine its own specific destination. Therefore, the modern sociological doctrine concerning legal abuse in civil private law, employing as a criterion the use of a subjective right contradicting the social-economic destination for which it was given (compare article 1 of the so-called Civil Codes of the Soviet Republics), cannot be reconciled with the foundations of civil law. It is a cautionary example of the undermining influence that the idea of droit social, in its overextension, exerts on civil private law.

# The contest over the concept of sovereignty[1]

**Introduction**

IN THE EVOLUTION of Jurisprudence and Political Science in the second half of the last century many tenets that used to be taken for unassailable truths, were cast into the melting pot of criticism. But among these none was of such signal importance as the concept of sovereignty.

Notably, since the two World Wars the idea that the dogma of sovereignty ought to be consigned to the scrap heap, both from a scientific and from a practical point of view, has increasingly taken hold in the democratic countries.

Undeniably the attack has been especially focused now on the consequences of the dogma in the area of international law, because international relations have more and more become the center of interest.

But in the theory of constitutional law and in the general theory of the state the opposition against this dogma had already begun to arise in the second half of the last century.

As early as 1888 the German doctor of constitutional law Hugo Preusz thought that the elimination of the concept of sovereignty from the dogmas of constitutional law would only be a small step forward on the road this science has in fact long since taken.[2]

Since then sociology of law has asserted itself as a participant in the controversy and several of its prominent exponents have pointed out that the important metamorphosis of the social-economic structure of Western society has increasingly ousted the state from its central position, which formerly seemed to be the basis of the doctrine of sovereign power.

Lastly, one of the well-known proponents of neo-Scholastic philosophy, Jacques Maritain, has also made his stand against this dogma. In a recent article, "The Concept of Sovereignty," he declared: "The two concepts of sovereignty and absolutism have been forged together on the same anvil. They must be scrapped together."[3]

---

1 Rectorial address, delivered on the occasion of the 70th anniversary of the Free University on 20 October 1950. This oration – considerably enlarged – was published in Dutch by J. H. Paris, Amsterdam: *De Strijd om het souvereiniteitsbegrip in de moderne Rechts- en Staatsleer* (The contest over the concept of sovereignty in modern Jurisprudence and Political Science) (62 pp.).

2 *Gemeinde, Staat, Reich als Gebietskörpershaften*, p.135.

3 *The American Political Science Review*, vol. XLIV (1950), no 2 p.343.

That, in spite of these combined attacks, the concept of sovereignty had by no means been eliminated from jurisprudence and political science became evident from the forcible plea Herman Heller made for its complete rehabilitation (1927), a plea that became a fierce arraignment of the tendencies aimed at the undermining of this fundamental concept.[1] Also, the Viennese professor Alfred Verdrosz, once an adherent of Kelsen's Reine Rechtslehre (pure doctrine of law) and, as such, a fierce opponent of the traditional conception of the authoritative sovereign state, accepted the latter in his book on international law (published in 1937) as the necessary foundation of the law of nations.

On the whole it may be said that in dogmatic jurisprudence the doctrine of sovereignty still predominates, even though there is a tendency to avoid its extreme consequences in international relations.

Before the tribunal of science, one would certainly not be justified in taking a stand in this topical contest before realizing the many-sided part that the traditional concept of sovereignty has played in jurisprudence and political science since the 16th century, and the problems that would present themselves if it were eliminated.

In the second place it is an undeniable duty of both science and politics to inquire whether the currents that are asserted to oppose the doctrine of sovereignty have indeed disengaged themselves from it or only tend to enforce it again on science and practice in another form. As so often happens in controversies on normative concepts, terminological misunderstandings and obscurities may cloud scientific discussion.

Finally, for those who in studying science take their stand on the basis of the fundamentals of our University it is of paramount importance to ponder whether they can accept the way the problem is presented in the modern contest about the traditional concept of sovereignty, or whether those who start from the principles of the Reformation must follow essentially different lines of thought.

It does not seem out of place on this 70th anniversary of our University to draw your attention to these fundamental questions. In doing so I shall first of all review the original content and the further evolution of the doctrine of sovereignty since the 16th century when it made its entry into jurisprudence and political science.


### The History of the Dogma

*Bodin's concept of sovereignty and the humanistic doctrine of natural law*

Five years after the massacre of St Bartholomew, when Jean Bodin published his famous work Six livres de la Republique, in which he founded his conception of the state on the concept of sovereignty, he made an impact which became of revolutionary importance both for political science and positive law.

---

[1] H. Heller, *Die Souveranität* (1927).

Although he made use of the Romanized train of thought of early and late-mediaeval legists and although in the further elaboration of his concept of sovereignty he had a near precursor in AENEAS SYLVIUS, the counsellor of the Emperor FREDEDRICK III, none before him had declared sovereignty to be the essential characteristic of every state. The central idea of this concept of sovereignty was not contained in its definition in the Latin edition of Bodin's book: summa in cives ac subditos legibusque soluta potestas (supreme power over the citizens and subjects which is not bound by state law). This formula is often misunderstood on account of insufficient study of Bodin's theory from the original source. Bodin by no means maintained that the sovereign head of state was above all laws. He considered the sovereign, in explicit contradiction to Macchiavelli, to be subject to natural and divine law. He considered him, like any of his subjects, to be bound by treaties (contracts), which he, as opposed to medieval German conception, distinguished from laws as authoritative ordinances.

And although in his time there could not yet be any question of positive international law, as the concept of state had hardly dawned, it was certainly not in accordance with Bodin's doctrine of sovereignty to deny that the state was bound to treaties it had entered into. Only subjection to a higher worldly power is, according to him, incompatible with state-concept. Bodin did not even mean to raise the sovereign head of the state above the so-called lois fondamentales of absolute monarchy. According to him the French king is subjected to these fundamental laws in so far as they are inherent in the possession of the crown, notably to the Salic law of succession. The adage Princeps legibus solutus est (the Prince is above the law) was, as we all know, derived from the commentary on the lex Julia et Papia (I, iii, 31) by the Roman legist Ulpianus and was in late-Imperial times explained in terms of absolutism. It was commonly accepted in the post-glossarist school and the rising humanistic legal school of Alciat, Budé and Zasius. And, in opposition to the extreme absolutist conception, we find it, for example, defended in the legal school of Toulouse in the reign of Francis I. It was Zasius who started the (qualified) ethical conception, as it was afterwards defended by Bodin and by Calvin. So in this respect Bodin's concept of sovereignty was nothing new.

On the other hand the way in which he elaborated the concept of "supreme power" was epoch-making. According to him the unity and indivisibility of sovereignty does not allow for any restriction of its mandate, either in power or in task or in time. The Emperor of the Holy Roman Empire, whose sovereign power was much curtailed by the well-known Wahlkapitulationen, was therefore – greatly to the vexation of the German legists – denied the title of sovereign and consequently that of supreme head of state. The French king is not subordinate either to him or to the Pope. Mixed forms of government are inexorably rejected as being incompatible with the concept of sovereignty. But above all, this latter implies, according to Bodin, the absolute and only original competence for the creation of law within the territory of the state. The legislative power as the first and most important consequence of sovereignty does not allow for any other original authority for the creation of law.

The validity of custom is made absolutely dependent on direct or indirect recognition by statute law, and the same holds, by implication, for all direct creation of laws in different spheres of life that are contained within the territory of the state. The monopoly in the domain of the creation of law, which the Roman Emperors had not claimed before absolutist Byzantine times, is here proclaimed, as the natural outcome of sovereignty, to be the essential characteristic of any state whatsoever.

In its general application to the growing absolute state, this theory was to become a practical programme and dominate the whole concept of positive law for the next few centuries. Science was pressed into the service of politics, which aimed at complete demolition of medieval society.

On the collapse of the Carlovingian state, society in the Germanic countries had relapsed into a split-up undifferentiated condition, in which only the hierarchy of the organized church could bring about unity and coordination. Society presented a secular infra-structure and an ecclesiastical supra-structure, which in their mutual relation corresponded to the fundamental religious motive of Roman Catholicism (the predominating cultural power down to the 14th century): the nature-grace motive.

The secular infra-structure presented a variegated aspect of social corporations, which were cut on two patterns: the guild-pattern and the pattern of the mundium-relation, with many crossovers in between.

The guild-pattern was an artificial imitation of the primitive old-Germanic sib whilst the mundium-relation was a somewhat weakened imitation of the old-Germanic absolute domestic power: the mundium.

The first pattern was evolved in the medieval cities with their trade-guilds, and in the country in the free villages and Markgenossenschaften. The second took effect, more or less markedly, in all medieval relations and gradations of authority (Herrschaft), i.e. in the higher, medial and lower lordships (seigniories), the feudal relations, the Grundherrschaften, etc.

Governmental power could be traded in. In other words, it was a *res in commercio*, not a public office in the service of a *res publica*. The sovereign lords could freely dispose of it. Once in the hands of private persons or corporations it had become their inviolable right. Hence medieval autonomy always implied the exercise of governmental power on one's own authority, which did not change even with the rise of political estates. In this undifferentiated condition of society, in which the guilds covered all spheres of human life, a real state could not evolve.

The idea of the *res publica* only continued in the theory of the legists versed in Roman law and in Aristotelian-Thomistic philosophy. But it was not founded on contemporary social reality. In this state of affairs it is to be understood that Bodin, in his concept of sovereignty, claimed the exclusive control of the creation of law for the sovereign head of state. Medieval autonomy in the creation of law was indeed incompatible with the state-concept for the very reason that it was undifferentiated. In this situation every autonomous law-sphere that claimed an original competence-sphere did at the same time claim governmental power of its own, which turned against the idea of the *res publica*, as it did not recognize any limitation of the public interest.

But Bodin's doctrine of sovereignty, which was favorable to the policy of bureaucratic centralization of absolute monarchy, defeated its own objective, namely the monopolization of governmental power. As soon as the process of differentiation of society is carried through and the state has monopolized all governmental power, it turns out that at the same time the evolution of law is passing through a differentiation as well, which cannot possibly be pressed into the framework of the law-sphere of the state. The doctrine that all positive law finds its legal source in the will of the sovereign law-giver then proves to be a political dogma in the fullest sense of the word, a dogma that is at complete variance both with the general meaning of all law and with the rich structural variety of society.

It is the everlasting credit of the Calvinistic jurist Johannes Althusius that at a time which was scientifically quite ripe for this absolutist conception of state-law, he expounded a theory of the structure of society, founded on the recognition of a divine world-order, and the intrinsic character of the social orbits of life, in which it was pointed out that each of the latter has its lex propria and its own legal sphere, which cannot be derived from any other. It may be true that this doctrine of the "symbiosis" lacked the scientific apparatus for a deeper analysis of these social structures, i.e. that, in its legal construction of every form of human society from some sort of contract, it followed the uniform schematic methods of natural law and that it was not yet quite free from the hierarchical-universalistic views of medieval theories. But, whatever the case may be, it had emancipated itself from the Aristotelian-Scholastic theory, which only bestowed the autonomous competency for the creation of law on the so-called societates perfectae, namely the state and the church. And for that reason it could not resist Bodin's doctrine of sovereignty in the domain of secular law on principle.

Meanwhile, the future apparently lay with the latter. Science – legal theory and the theory of the state included – was increasingly affected by the modern humanistic philosophy with its religious root-principle of nature and freedom, the domination of the realities of nature by science, and the absolute autonomy of the free human personality in the domain of science, morals and religion.

The domination-motive gave rise to the classic-humanistic ideal of science, which proclaimed the methods of mathematics and natural science – the latter having been founded by Galileo and Newton – to be the universal mode of thought, on which a new theoretical picture of reality was designed, and which left no room for structural and natural differences founded on the order of creation.

It had been called into existence by the new motive of freedom but was, if carried through consistently, bound to collide with the latter. In a construction of reality modeled on the concepts of natural science no room was left for autonomy and freedom of the human personality.

Even in Bodin's political philosophy this scientific ideal – not yet consolidated in his time – began to make its influence felt. Science was pressed into the service of a policy that wanted to build up the state as a rational institution for the purpose of domination, after the demolition of the undifferentiated society of the Middle Ages.

This being the object, Bodin, in his political theory, wanted to develop the means to this end in a rigorously methodical, mathematical way.

It starts with a definition: "The state is the lawful government of several households and what they have in common, it having sovereign power."

And then Bodin declares: "We premise this definition, because in all things one must trace the principal object first, and only afterwards the means to attain it. Well then, the definition is nothing but the object of the matter under discussion; and if it is not well-founded, everything that is built on it, will collapse soon after."

But his definition was by no means the result of a conscientious inquiry into the inner nature and structure of the state-organism and of the other social spheres of life. It had been dictated by a political objective that ignored the divine world-order from which Althusius started, and only aimed at the complete domination of society by the instrument of the state.

Within the framework that had thus been determined by his political objective, Bodin's concept of sovereignty performed the following various functions, which we ought to remember in their mutual relation in order to be able to assess correctly their several pros and cons:

1. drawing the boundary lines between the state and all other political and non-political social spheres of life;
2. defining the concept of positive law as the certified will of the law-giver;
3. defining the relation between the different orbits of competence in the creation of law, all of which are to be dependent on the only original competence, i.e. that of the sovereign state by virtue of its legislative power.

The humanistic doctrine of natural law, founded by Hugo Grotius, accepted Bodin's concept of sovereignty. It was also pressed into the service of the policy of demolition and renovation. More geometrico, by the analysis of society as it presents itself into its "elements," i.e. the individuals, and by the synthetic construction of the desired new society from these social elements with the help of a juridical social contract, it wanted to build up a new social and legal order. In order to make Bodin's concept of sovereignty acceptable to the humanistic ideas of liberty and autonomy, the humanistic doctrine of natural law constructed the state from a social contract between naturally free and equal individuals, mostly complemented by an authority- and subjection-contract, and in Pufendorf even by a third contract about the form of government. In Hobbes' Leviathan and in Rousseau's so-called infallible and all-powerful volonté général the concept of sovereignty got its most consistently absolutist elaboration.

Like Bodin's concept of sovereignty, his conception of the relation between legislation and custom was also accepted. The indigenous customary law had under the test of the classic-Roman tradition of the ius naturale et gentium become a ius iniquum, a bulwark of feudal society, which was doomed to ruin.

In the new order no other law was permitted besides civil law and the ius publicum, that is to say the two frameworks of state-law. For that purpose positive law was to be elaborated in exhaustive codes.

It was not until the British philosopher John Locke appeared on the scene that there arose in the doctrine of natural law a reaction against the absolutist concept of sovereignty, i.e. from the angle of the humanistic concept of freedom.

The liberal idea of the constitutional state, developed by Locke, led to a rigorous distinction between state and society while the theory of the division of power, which was presently to get its definite shape in Montesquieu's doctrine of the trias politica, was also bound to result in the inner decay of the dogma of sovereignty.

*The historical interpretation of the concept of sovereignty and the doctrine of state-sovereignty*

At the time of the Restoration (i.e. after the destruction of the Napoleonic empire), the doctrine of sovereignty takes quite a new turn, because it now joins up with the principle of legitimacy and the so-called monarchical principle, and fundamentally denies every contractual construction as propounded by the doctrine of natural law.

Whereas in the preceding period the problem of sovereign power had been tackled from the viewpoint of natural law, quite detached from the historical past, and whereas only a formulation in accordance with that point of view had been applied to the absolutist or to the more liberal-constitutional tendencies of the time, now, in accordance with the conservative historical mode of thought of the Restoration movement, full stress is laid on the real or imaginary historical rights of the dynasties that had been dethroned by the revolution. The pre-revolutionary position of the Bourbons in France served as a model. In the introduction to the chapter on Louis XVIII, which preamble was drafted by Beugnot, the latter provided the standard formula that passed into the constitutions of several German states and was proclaimed to be the unassailable dogmatic starting-point for the deduction of the constitutional status of the princes in art.57 of the Final Treaty of Vienna.

In this formulation the sovereignty of the king was not based on the constitution, but inversely the constitution was granted as a charter by the sovereign prince by virtue of his supposed fullness of power, which was considered to be founded on historical rights. And the required cooperation of the estates or the parliament for the exercise of legislative power rested on the voluntary self-restriction of sovereign power.

On the one hand the concept of sovereignty – for that matter in accordance with Hobbes's and Rousseau's conceptions – was thus tightened up even from that of Bodin's conception. Bodin considered royal sovereignty legally bound to the lois fondamentales of the realm, which were independent of that sovereignty. However, on the other hand the historical views of Restoration times struck the first blow to the principle of Bodin's doctrine as regards the monopoly of the sovereign law-giver in the domain of the creation of the law. This came about under the influence of an irrationalistic and universalistic turn in the humanistic freedom motive as it was elaborated in post-Kantian idealism (notably in Schelling's transcendental idealism).

The absolute value of individuality was turned against the over-strained notions of uniform generality; and in opposition to the apotheosis of the individual in the individualistic mode of thought of the exponents of natural law, the community was now enthroned.

Society was no longer considered an aggregate of free and equal individuals, but an organic whole with parts, and the free and autonomous individual personality of a person was looked on in the light of that person's membership in an equally individual natural community, on which a collective personality was conferred.

This new conception of the humanistic freedom motive also asserted itself in science. The standard mode of thought borrowed from physical science was ousted everywhere by a historical way of approach, which aimed at understanding the individual in its individual-historical relations in accordance with modes of thought in the spiritual branches of science. Over against the rationalistic belief that one could construct political and legal order on an unalterable model which would be in accordance with the doctrine of natural law and ready-made for all times and all peoples, independent of the historical past, all stress was now laid on the organic character of the historical development of a culture that has its true source in the individual national character or Volksgeist. Thus a new ideal of science arose, which, by making the historical aspect of society absolute, led to an exaggerated historical vision (or "historicistic" vision, if you like) of reality.

And this historical mode of thought was, of course, bound to turn against the traditional conception of positive law as a product of the sovereign will of the law-giver.

The Historical School of law, founded by Fr. Carl von Savigny, who proclaimed law to be a phenomenon of historical evolution that originally springs organically (i.e. without being intentionally created) from the individual spirit or conviction of the people, totally broke with the former rationalistic conception of the relation between statute law and customary law.

Over against the doctrine of natural law was placed that of folk-law (Volksrecht) in its historical evolution. That folk-law, they held, did not spring from the will of the sovereign law-giver but from the historical law-mindedness of the people.

Folk-law at first reveals itself in the Uebung as customary law but when social relations are becoming more complicated, it gets a technical organ in the class of lawyers, and its technical form in the Juristenrecht. In relation to this, legislation has only a secondary task. If this train of thought were consistently carried through, the traditional concept of sovereignty would have to be discarded as a necessary element in the definition of positive law.

However, it was not the Romanistic, but the Germanistic wing of the Historical School, led by its two principal exponents Georg Beseler and Otto Gierke, which began to draw conclusions from the doctrine of folk-law that turned out to be fatal for the traditional concept of sovereignty. If all law is, as von Savigny taught, a historical product of the individual Volksgeist the reception of the Roman law in the Germanic countries must be considered as a denaturation of the healthy development of the Germanic legal institutions. The spirit of Roman civil law, stigmatized as being individualistic, was, just as the absolutist concept of government of the Roman imperium, quite antagonistic to the "social, corporative" foundations of Germanic law. The study of the Germanic corporate system led to a more sociological view of jurisprudence and the Germanists proclaimed, in diametrical opposition to the Romanist Puchta, the autonomy of corporations to be a formal original source of law. They discovered internal corporate law as being Sozialrecht, which was unknown to classical tradition.

At first, under the influence of the historical mode of thought, this Germanistic rush threatened to undermine completely the foundations of civil law and of the state-concept. But Gierke saw the danger in time and compromised with the idea of natural law. The doctrine of the rights of individuals (in the classic tradition of the ius naturale et gentium the foundation of civil law) could not be sacrificed to the Germanic concept of folk-law which bound the whole legal status of the individual to the undifferentiated social corporations. The Individual-recht was to be maintained as an independent sphere of law beside the newly discovered Sozialrecht of the corporations. The classic concept of the state as a sovereign *res publica* could also not be allowed to succumb to the undifferentiated corporative principle of Germanic law.

However, Gierke wanted to replace the conception of the bureaucratic sovereign state, derived from the idea of the Roman Empire, which conception was pregnantly expressed in Bodin's identification of the *res publica* with the government, by an "organic" idea of the state, in which the government was to be recognized as an essential organ of an organization of the state that comprised both the government and the people.

This organized state is, according to him, just as any other social corporate sphere, a real "spiritual organism" with a personality of its own. But it is a gegliederte Gemeinschaft, in which both the legal subjectivity of the individual citizens and that of the narrower corporate spheres, integrated into the whole of the state, remain untouched. The Germanic Genossenschaftsprinzip could in this way successfully impact the modern idea of a constitutional state.

Sovereignty in its fullest sense then could not belong to the government or to the people, but only to the state as a whole. The government can only exercise sovereign power as an organ of the essentially corporate state.

Thus the doctrine of the sovereignty of the state was born, which in the form propounded by Gierke was in many respects of a higher conception than those of Gerber, Laband and Jellinek, who are generally considered the typical representatives of this doctrine. And it was notably superior to Bodin's doctrine of sovereignty, which was not based on a truly corporate conception of the state.

Meanwhile, the new doctrine of the sovereignty of the state, in so far as it was really in accordance with the thought of the Historical School, held all the germs which were destined to completely undermine the traditional humanistic concept of sovereignty.

Since the theory of folk-law had led to the doctrine of the autonomous creation of law in the different social spheres, the concept of sovereignty, when elaborated consistently, could no longer have the characteristic quality of being the only original competency for the creation of positive law.

So the question was bound to arise as to what role it could still play in the definition of the state.

Gierke himself still stuck to Bodin's conception that sovereignty was to be considered an essential quality of any state. The latter, in his opinion, is distinguished from all other social spheres of life as a "sovereign organization of power," which is not to be taken in the sense of Genossenschaft, but of Gebietskörperschaft, because the first concept applied in his system only to the non-political spheres.

Thus the concept of sovereignty had unmistakably been transferred from the legal sphere to the historical-political sphere of power and had become a historical category instead of one that belonged to the domain of natural law.

This conclusion had been emphatically drawn by Gerber, Laband and Jellinek from the rupture with the conception of the doctrine of natural law. And from this it further followed that they, in contradistinction to Gierke, no longer considered sovereignty an essential characteristic of the state, but also acknowledged the existence of non-sovereign states.

As soon, however, as the concept of sovereignty was transferred from the sphere of natural law to the historical sphere of power, a problem presented itself for which the doctrine of the sovereignty of the state could not offer a satisfactory solution, namely the question about the relation of the sovereign power of the state to "law."

The problem, in this form, had been put in a decidedly uncritical way. For "state" and "law" are not to be compared in this way. The sphere of law is, among many others, only a modal aspect of human society. The state, on the other hand, is a real corporate sphere of social life, which in this capacity functions in all aspects, so necessarily also in its juridical aspect. And the typical structures of the differentiated spheres of social life (state, church, trade, family, etc.) introduce into the juridical aspect that typical variety which makes it impossible to speak of "law" as such, without further social qualification.

Thus public law and civil law are the two characteristic legal spheres of the state, which differ fundamentally from the internal ecclesiastical law, the internal law of trades and industries, etc., and can never be placed in opposition to the state.

Gierke, however, went wrong in stating the problem, so that he could not offer a sound solution.

According to him "state" and "law" are "two autonomous and specifically different sides of communal life. The former manifests itself in the powerful pursuance of chosen communal goals and culminates in political action while the latter reveals itself in the delimitation of action-spheres appropriate for the will bound by these spheres and reaches its peak in legal acknowledgement (when it is accepted as law)."[1]

This untenable juxtaposition of state and law showed the inner conflict between the concept of sovereignty rooted in the humanistic power- or domination-motive and the folk-law theory of the Historical School, which was based on the humanistic freedom motive and was only prepared to acknowledge law as the free and autonomous expression of the "conviction of the people."

In other words, the problem was born of the humanistic basic motive of nature and freedom itself and Gierke only tried in a dialectical way to unite the two antagonistic motives of domination and freedom; because giving a positive form to law, according to him, needs the sovereign state. Conversely, the sovereign power of the state, in order not to degenerate into despotism, is in need of law for its foundation.

However, it could not be denied that the concept of sovereignty clashed with Gierke's doctrine of the social corporate spheres and their autonomous creation of law. Gierke's disciple, Hugo Preusz, starting from this doctrine and the folk-law theory of the Historical School, was the first to eliminate on principle the concept of sovereignty. The latter is according to him the necessary correlate of the individualistic concept of personality with both originating from Roman law. In contrast to the absolutist state, the modern constitutional state has developed from the Germanic legal principle of the autonomous Genossenschaft. And the concept of sovereignty does not suit this constitutional state any longer. If the state is, as Gierke has expounded, an organic corporate person among a series of organic corporate persons, which can be integrated as members into more comprehensive "persons" of that kind, the problem of the composing parts of the Germanic federal state and of the insertion of that state into the organization of the nations on the basis of international law can also be solved. Everywhere the concept of sovereignty stood in the way of the right insight into this matter.

But this concept of sovereignty is not so easily done away with. From the outset it had played a far more varied role than how it came across in Preusz' speculations. The Germanistic wing of the Historical School had posited the autonomy of the corporate social spheres as an original formal source of law

---

[1] *Die Grundbegriffe des Staatsrechts und die neuesten Staatsrechtstheorien* (Tübingen, Mohr, 1915), p.105: "zwei selbständige und spezifisch verschiedene Seiten des Gemeinlebens. Jenes manifestiert sich in der machtvollen Durchführung gewollter Gemeinzwecke und kulminirt in der politischen That, dieses offenbart sich in der Absteckung von Handlungssphären für die von ihm gebundenen Willen und gipfelt im rechtlichen Erkennen (für Recht erkennen)."

but had failed to mention a material criterion for the demarcation of the original orbits of competency of the state and the other spheres of life in the domain of the creation of law. Which of them would have to give way in case of conflict?

The doctrine of sovereignty had at least given an unequivocal answer. And Gierke himself did not know how to replace it by another. He too contended that no autonomous corporation law could assert itself against the sovereign will of the state.

The concept of sovereignty cannot be eliminated unless another solution can be offered for the problem concerning the mutual relation of the original orbits of competency in the domain of the creation of law.

And the paramount question in this matter is whether one considers this an intrinsic problem of law or a historical question of power.

The traditional doctrine of sovereignty had essentially always put it as a question of power, for the construction of the sovereign power of the government from a voluntary contract – as the doctrine of natural law had proposed – had likewise been nothing but a juridical mask for the humanistic power- and domination- motive.

This had created a conflict between might and right that could not be allayed either in Gierke's "dialectical" way or by Jellinek's well-known doctrine of the voluntary self-restriction of the will of the state by law.

### *The doctrine of the sovereignty of law (Rechtssouveranität) and its presumed victory over the traditional dogma of sovereignty*

This conflict seemed to be avoided by the doctrine of the sovereignty of law, which in three variants, namely the psychological one of Krabbe, the normlogical one of Kelsen and the legal-sociological one of Duguit and Gurvitch, turned against the traditional concept of sovereignty, no matter whether it presented itself in the form of the sovereignty of government, of the people, or of the state.

In reality, however, the doctrine of the sovereignty of law has not in any way overcome the antimonies of the traditional concept of sovereignty. It wants us to believe that the problems for which the latter seemed to give a solution, would vanish in thin air, if only, instead of the state or the people or the government, impersonal legal order were proclaimed sovereign. But legal order is only the law- or norm-facet of the juridical aspect of human society, and the great variety in structure which characterizes our modern, much differentiated society, is, as we observed before, also bound to be expressed in its juridical aspect.

So the doctrine of sovereignty of law cannot escape a definition of the mutual relation of the competency of the state and that of the other social spheres of life. For which of the variants of law could rightfully claim sovereignty? Constitutional law, international law, the internal laws of trades and industries, ecclesiastical law?

Whatever one's choice may be, one will always be obliged to endow one of the social spheres of life with an absolute competency and sovereignty. But an absolute competency can never be a real legal power, as it does not allow for any real demarcation by law.

Thus the doctrine of the sovereignty of law in its turn collides with the general character of all law and is obliged in the end to resolve the problem of juridical competency into a historical question of power.

And yet this doctrine owed its very origin to the attempt to save the independence of the law over against power!

Recently, Gurvitch (*Sociology of Law*, 1947) tried to escape the difficulty by attributing absolute sovereignty to the unorganized "supra-functional" community of the nation and the international community of peoples which he calls the all-embracing infra-structures of society. These would in an absolutely variable way demarcate the orbits of competence of all differentiated "functional" communities like state, church, industrial organizations, etc.

The supra-functional sovereign communities are here thought of as being "undifferentiated." In them the idea of "law" would be embodied "in all its ways," whereas in the "functional" communities only special aspects of this law-idea would be expressed.

But there are no unorganized communities with a supra-functional character. The undifferentiated spheres of primitive society are always organized and they are doomed to disappear when the process of differentiation sets in. Hence Gurvitch is compelled again to proclaim a differentiated corporate sphere to be the exclusive representative and binding interpreter of the absolutely sovereign legal order of the all-embracive "supra-functional communities."

In these periods of state-absolutism in which personal liberty and the liberty of other spheres of life run the greatest danger, that representative, according to Gurvitch, must be the state itself, which now, for its usurping interference with the original orbits of competency of the other spheres of life, even receives the sanction of "sovereign law"!

Thus in this theory of the sovereignty of law too, sovereignty swallows up law so that the power-motive predominates over the freedom motive.

### The traditional concept of sovereignty and the doctrine of sovereignty in its proper orbit

Surveying once more the evolution of the concept of sovereignty in humanistic legal and political science, I think I may state the following: in all its manifestations, including also in the doctrine of the sovereignty of law, the concept of sovereignty implied the denial of the existence of original, materially and juridically defined orbits of competence of the state and the other spheres of life.

Original spheres of competence in this material and juridical sense can never be based on an order of positive law, because any formation of positive law as such presupposes the original competence or jural power to this end. Only derived competency can be based on positive law and consequently have a necessarily variable foundation.

Irrespective of how far one ascends in any possible hierarchy of derived competencies formed according to the rules of positive law, in the end one will arrive at the original competency from which the said hierarchy itself has been derived. What then is the basis of this original jural power as the presupposition of all positive law?

This jural power can only be founded on and be materially defined by the inner nature, by the internal structural principle of the social sphere within which it is executed, which principle is independent of any human discretion. As an original jural power – not derived from another temporal sphere of life – it may be called sovereign, provided this concept of sovereignty is immediately circumscribed by "in its proper orbit." And then at the same time it becomes the radical opposite of the concept of sovereignty construed by humanistic theories. For, in spite of all attempts to provide the latter concept with a juridical basis or at least some legal demarcation, it broke theoretically with inner necessity through the boundaries of the original social spheres of competency, and at the same time through the modal confines of the law.

"Sovereignty in its proper orbit" is not some vague political slogan, the cry of a special Christian political party. It is deeply rooted in the whole real order of things, and is not to be ignored with impunity. For it is the expression of the sovereign divine will and wisdom of the Creator, who created all things after their own kind and set their constant structural boundaries in the order of temporal reality. And it is he who maintained this temporal order of reality even after the fall of humankind, to reveal it in the redemption by Jesus Christ in all its religious fullness of meaning: the focussing of all temporal reality on the loving service of the glorification of God.

In other words, sovereignty in its proper orbit is a universal ontological principle, which gets its special legal expression only in the juridical aspect of reality. It reveals two different givens in the structure of reality: (i) the mutual irreducibility of the different aspects of reality; (ii) their indissoluble intertwinement and connection in the temporal order of reality.

For only in their indissoluble connectedness can they reveal their irreducible uniqueness.

This holds both for the structures of the different modal aspects of reality,[1] which in general structure the unique coherence of the latter, and the typical structures of individual totalities in which these modal aspects are united in their integral connectedness and are grouped and individualized into an individual whole in characteristically different ways.

---

[1] In my work *De Wijsbegeerte der Wetsidee* (The Philosophy of the Law-Idea) the following modal aspects of empirical reality are distinguished: The aspect of quantity (number), the space-aspect, the aspect of motion, [this aspect was only introduced in 1950 – DFMS] the energetic (physico-chemical) aspect, the biotic aspect, the psychical aspect of feeling, the logical or analytical aspect, the historical aspect, the symbolic or linguistic aspect, the aspect of social intercourse, the economic aspect, the aesthetic aspect, the jural aspect, the moral aspect and the faith aspect.

All jural relations – in whatever typical social structure of totality (that of the state, the church, trade, international relations, etc.) they may present themselves – are as jural relations determined by the general modal structure of the juridical aspect of reality.

In this modal structure the whole order and connectedness of the different aspects are expressed in an irreducible modus. As I set out and argued in detail in my De Wijsbegeerte der Wetsidee, [NC] Vol.II, it is built up from a nuclear moment, which warrants the irreducibility of the aspect, and from a series of other structural moments, some of which (the so-called analogies) maintain the inner coherence of the jural aspect with all those modalities occupying an earlier position in the order of aspects, while others (the so-called anticipations) maintain connection with those positioned later in the order of aspects although all of them are qualified by the nuclear moment of the jural aspect.[1]

Among the analogical moments in the modal structure of this aspect, the juridical competency or jural power takes an essential place. It is the prerequisite for all human molding of the principles of law into concrete form, through which these principles are elaborated into positive norms of law.

Competency is jural power, and in this strong term (i.e. jural power) the indissoluble connection between the juridical and the historical aspect of reality is expressed. For power (or control) is the modal nuclear moment of the historical aspect which is the aspect pertaining to cultural development.

Jural power is not power in the original sense of history. It is only a historical analogy in the modal structure of law, which is always qualified by the modal nuclear moment of the juridical aspect. But it is founded in historical relations of power, and can never be independent of the latter.

Essentially this juridical competency is never absolute or exclusive. It is premised on a number of original orbits of competency that exist in jural relations of mutual circumscription and balance. For as in all fundamental concepts of jurisprudence, there is to be found in the concept of competency also a numerical analogy, in which the inner coherence between the juridical and the quantitative aspect is expressed. Jural life in which only one jural subject would function is no more possible than true jural life in which only one original orbit of competency for the formation of law would be given. Even in a still undifferentiated society this is impossible.

From this it is once again evident that the traditional concept of sovereignty must necessarily collide with the modal sovereignty-in-its-orbit of the juridical aspect of social reality.

Because in the theoretical conception of reality, from which this notion of sovereignty started, there was not even any room for the modal structures of the different aspects of social reality, it could a fortiori have no place for the typical structures of the different social spheres since the latter cannot be un-

---

[1] *Editorial note* (DFMS): Dooyeweerd later on explained the inter-modal coherence between the different aspects by grouping both retrocipations and anticipations together as analogical structural moments. Systematically one should therefore distinguish between retrocipatory and anticipatory analogies (cf. A New Critique of Theoretical Thought, [NC] Vol.II, p.75).

derstood without being based on the former. So the concept of sovereignty was proclaimed the essential characteristic of the state, because the internal structural principle of the latter (and with it its inner nature) had been eliminated.

Well, it is exactly these structures of the social spheres of life that lend to each of the original spheres of competency their typical material content and delimitation.

In the order of reality they are founded as structural principles, but they can only be realized by being molded into concrete form by humankind.

The results of this fashioning human activity are the social forms, which always have a historical foundation and vary throughout with the historical evolution of society.

The typical structural principles of the social spheres of life, on the other hand, have a constant and invariable character, because they determine the inner nature of these spheres. The inner nature of the state or of the church-institute do not change in the course of time, but only the social forms in which these social institutions are realized. These social forms are the nodal points of the intertwinement of the orbits of life, which are so entirely different from each other in their internal structure and nature.

But as each of the modal structures of the aspects in their mutual connectedness retains its modal sovereignty in its proper orbit, so each of the typical structures of the differentiated social spheres in their mutual intertwinement maintains its typical sovereignty in its proper orbit and thus, for example in the juridical aspect it maintains its original sphere of competency in the domain of the creation of law.

The state has no exceptional position in this respect. It has only sovereignty in its proper orbit. However, this does not do away with the fact that its original jural power is of quite a different kind.

In conformity with its internal structure, the state must be characterized as a territorial and institutional corporation of public law, a public juridical community of government and subjects on the historical basis of a monopolistic organization of the power of the sword. For, as with any differentiated social structure, that of the state is also typified by two modal functions acting in different modal aspects, the first of which is called the typical "qualifying function" or "directive function," the second the "typical basic function."

The internal structural principle is also expressed in the other aspects of the life of the state: the moral, the economic, the symbolic, the sensory, the biotic aspect, etc.

The directive function of the state – in contrast to all other spheres of life – has its place in the juridical aspect of social reality. This means that the state, acting as such in the domain of the creation of law, has no original competency for the creation of law that will serve some non-juridical destination.

All law is specific law, i.e. ius specificum, if, in in conformity with the internal societal structure within which it obtains, it typically serves a meta-juridical destination, such as the economically qualified internal law of trades, or for example, the internal ecclesiastical law, which is qualified by its faith-destination.

The law, framed by the state, on the other hand, is by its very nature ius commune.

In accordance with its special modal structure, law shows a correlation of what we call coordinational and communal relations, because in any social relation, whatever its typical structure may be, this correlation is inherent.

In the partner-relation, the subjects do not act as members of a whole, but are juxtaposed, next to or even over against each other. In the communal relation, on the other hand, they are united as members of a whole that comprises all of them.

In typical state-law we therefore meet with the correlation of two typical spheres, namely civil law and public law, the first being a state-law regulating the civil coordinational relations of individuals as such, the latter being an inner social law of the state as a public community.

These are the two original spheres of competency of the state in the domain of the creation of law, which are materially demarcated by their inner structure and uniqueness.

In accordance with their typical constitution, internal trade law or internal ecclesiastical law cannot assume the character of public law or civil law.

Non-state law, it is true, will, as ius specificum, be subjected to a typical binding in civil and public law, and therefore it would seem as if the state had absolute sovereignty as to the creation of law. These deceptive appearances become even stronger when the internal structural principles of the social spheres and their typical legal spheres are not recognized while the juridical forms in which positive law is laid down, such as acts, ordinances, contracts, statutes, jurisdiction, etc. receive all the attention exclusively.

For just as social forms proved to be the nodal points of the mutual intertwinement of social orbits, so in the juridical aspect the formal sources of law are the nodal points of the mutual intertwinement of the original orbits of competency. But even in the closest intertwinements each of these spheres maintains its sovereignty in its own proper orbit.

This is neither the time or the place to elaborate further on all this here. Allow me, therefore, to conclude my reflections on the concept of sovereignty with a final word.

In the course of my argument the fundamental objections I have set forth against this concept in its traditional interpretation have a deeper background, i.e. in the total theoretical conception of reality from which it was born.

The theoretical conception of reality from which the different branches of science take their starting point is never neutral towards religion but is intrinsically dominated by the religious basic-motive through which scientific thought-activity gets its central driving force.

Here lies the inner and necessary point of contact between religion and science.

POLITICAL PHILOSOPHY

As our University expands, the inner reformation of our theoretical view of reality becomes more and more urgent.

For it is not steeds and horsemen that will lead us to victory in the effort to realize the ideal of our institution's founder, but it is only and finally the inner motive-power of the Scriptural basic-motive of the Reformation: that of the creation, the fall of humankind and our redemption by Jesus Christ, which must also radically change our theoretical vision of reality, if we want to aim at a science that is not merely scholastically accommodated, but really reformed in an intrinsic Christian sense.

# Selections from A New Critique of Theoretical Thought on the State[1]

*The empirical data concerning the State's character*
The radical typical and genotypical structural principle of the body politic cannot be traced apart from its realization in the development of human society.[2]

In this respect we must establish that a real State-institution does not appear before the destruction of the political power concentrated in the primitive undifferentiated tribal and gentilitial organizations. There is a radical difference between the latter and a real body politic appearing from the undeniable fact that they are incompatible with one another. Wherever a real State arose, its first concern was the destruction of the tribal and gentilitial political power or, if the latter had already disappeared, the struggle against the undifferentiated political power-formations in which authoritative, and private proprietary relations were mixed with each other. Irrespective of its particular governmental form, the State-institution has always presented itself as a *res publica*, an institution of the public interest, in which political authority is considered a public office, not a private property.

In this respect there appears to be a fundamental and radical difference between a real body politic, and the ancient Asiatic empires, the Merovingian kingdom and the medieval feudal kingdoms, which lacked the republican character.

It is extremely confusing that the term republic is used to indicate a non-monarchical form of government. In common speech it is unavoidable that the same words have very different meanings. But in the general theory of the State this is indefensible. The erroneous opposition between republics and monarchies is here only caused by the fact that the rise of a real State-institution in Greece and Rome occurred in a nonmonarchical form and our political terminology is of a Greco-Roman origin. In addition, the undifferentiated conception of political authority, as the personal property of the rulers, mostly maintained itself in monarchies. But these historical facts cannot justify a scientific use of the term republic in a sense which has nothing to

---

1 Cf. NC III:411-451.
2 *Editorial note* (DFMS): According to Dooyeweerd a *radical-type* always has a typical foundational and qualifying function. The state, for example – as will be explained below – has its foundational function in the *cultural-hitorical aspect* and it finds its qualifying aspect in the *jural mode or reality*. Insofar as the peculiar properties of a radical type are an expression of the of the *inner nature* of an individual whole, Dooyeweerd refers to them as *geno types* or *primary types*. When these peculiar properties are co-determined by forms of interlacement of a different radical- or geno-type Dooyeweerd speaks of *variability-types* or *pheno-types*. Cf. NC III:93.

do with its proper meaning. A real State with a monarchical form of government is by nature a monarchical republic. A kingdom like the Merovingian empire which was nothing but a *res regia* lacks the character of a real State-institution. The historicistic view, which levels out these radical differences and speaks of gentilitial, tribal and feudal "States," may not be called "empirical" since it ignores undeniable empirical states of affairs in order to carry through its historicist prejudice.

Even from a logical point of view this use of the concept State is indefensible since it is contradictory to subsume under one and the same notion characteristics which exclude one another in an analytical sense. It is true that the State belongs to a particular *radical type* of societal relationships which may also include organized communities of a different genotype. But in this case the term State may not be applied to this radical type but only to a specific genotype of the former.[1]

The adherents of MAX WEBER's ideal-typical method will readily agree that their ideal-typical concept of the State is only applicable to the modern bodies politic. But this by no means implies an abandonment of the historicist prejudice concerning the transient[2] character of the State's inner nature. The genotype State cannot be defined from a historical point of view only, since it is a real structure of individuality, which, as such, embraces the integral horizon of modal experiential aspects.

### *The typical foundational function of the State*

If we now try to trace the structural principle of individuality of the State from the empirical data mentioned above, it is in the first place necessary to devote our attention to the typical foundational function in this structure.

That this foundational function must be of a typical historical character cannot be doubted. For it appeared that the State-institution is based upon a typical concentration of power which has its historical condition in the destruction of the independent political power formations inherent in undifferentiated social organizations. But what type of individuality is revealed in this political organization of power proper to the State?

From our ample analysis of the modal structure of the historical aspect in the second Volume we know that power, in its nuclear modal sense, allows of widely different individuality types.[3] The historical power of the Christian Church has an entirely different individuality-structure from that of a modern or an ancient State, and the power of each of them is structurally entirely different from that of a modern large-scale industrial undertaking, or that of a sci-

---

1. *Editorial note* (DFMS): The technical term *radical* used by Dooyeweerd in this context actually refers to his systematic distinction between (functional) *aspects* and *entities*. Different kinds of entities are distinguished on the basis of particular characterizing functions. They are called the *foundational* and the *qualifying function* of an entity (process or societal institution). Entities qualified by the same modal aspect (function) belong to the same *radical type*. The idea of *geno-types* account for differences between entities belonging to the same radical type.

2. *Editorial note* (DFMS): the original text reads: "changeable."

3. Cf. [NC] Vol.II, part I, pp.196 ff.

entific or of an aesthetic "school," *etc.*

In an undifferentiated organized community different individuality-structures of historical power may be interlaced in one and the same organizational form, but the *State,* as such, has a differentiated structure. Therefore its internal power-formation can no longer display an undifferentiated structure. We must keep in mind that we are looking for the typical foundational function of this societal institution which is the original substratum for the type of individuality of its leading or qualifying function. In whatever way we consider the matter, this foundational function of the genotype "State" can nowhere else be found but in an *internal monopolistic organization of the power of the sword over a particular cultural area within territorial boundaries*.

The reader should remember that this typical historical structural function may in no way be naturalistically misinterpreted. According to its *modal* meaning it is a normative structural function implying a *task,* a *vocation* which can be realized in a better or a worse way. There has never existed any State whose internal structure in the last instance was not based on organized armed power, at least claiming the ability to break any armed resistance on the part of private persons or organizations within its territory.

### The myth of blood-relationship in the German national-socialistic ideology of the "third Empire," and the typical foundational function in the structure of the State

In the political mythology of German national-socialism it was suggested that the community of blood and soil was the real foundation of "the third Empire." But even in this case the internal structure of the State was not supposed to have a typical biotic foundation in a common descent. The starting point of this view was the community of the German people as including the entire individual personality, all the special structural communities and relationships such as the State, the Church, industry, political party, youth organization, *etc.* These societal units were viewed as differentiations of the primary community of the people, although the State was finally considered to be its totalitarian *political form of organization.* Only for this "community of the people" was postulated a "community of blood" in the myth of the race.

This myth was not to be understood in the sense of a naturalistic racial theory. This must be evident to anyone who has realized that the background of this racial ideology was found in the irrationalist-historistic view of life and the world[1] entertained by German national socialism.[2] There was a reminiscence of irrationalistic Romanticism in the Ger-

---

[1] A view of life and the world as such is not a theory. This is an important point in this context. Cf. [NC] Vol.I Prolegomena, pp.156 ff. In his famous article in the *Enciclopedia Italiana* on the *Dottrina fascists* (1932), MUSSOLINI made the following observation as to fascism as a view of life and the world: "To fascism the cosmos is not that material world in which man is led by a law of nature," and: "Fascism is a mental attitude born out of the general reaction of our century to the superficial and materialistic positivism of the 19th century." This could be taken over literally by German national socialism.

[2] Thus WALTER HAMEL in his treatise cited below.

man national socialist ideology of the "pure racial community of blood of the German people," though it was deprived of any Romantic idealism. It was connected with the old Germanic myth of a common descent claimed for all Germanic peoples. The mythology of Italian fascism, on the other hand, consciously fell back on the old idea of the eternal Roman empire.[1] Therefore Italian fascism was *State-minded*,[2] whereas German national-socialism was *folk-minded*, an ideological difference on which the German nazists laid strong emphasis.[3]

If full justice to such myths is to be done, they should be interpreted from the irrationalist-historicistic spirit of the view of life and the world in the background. Their essential aim was to elevate the historically developed nationality (the "cultural race," or the "national State" respectively) to a "spiritual power." This power should be actual and always again be actualized and assume all-absorbing validity in the conviction of the people.[4] The political myths also aimed at exorcising powers that were alleged to be a menace to the deified nationality.

In the German national socialist *theory* of the State it was realized that the structure of the State, as such, cannot be derived from a national community as a "community of blood." This is evident, for instance, from WALTER HAMEL's book *Das Wesen des Staatsgebietes* (1933), in which the State and the people are explicitly conceived to be connected in a dialectical tension. The State, as such, is *historically* founded in the sovereign control of a "political territory" (*"politischen Raum"*). This *"Bodemgemeinschaft"* (territorial community) is explicitly qualified as the adversary of the people (*"Widersacher des Volkes"*), which, however, always strives after a dialectical connection with the "community of blood."[5]

Of course, it is perfectly true that a State cannot maintain itself long if it is not rooted in the moral "conviction of the people," at least of the ruling groups of such a people. The State will be shortlived if it is divided and torn by internal

---

1 Cf. MUSSOLINI's statement in his quoted article on the *Doctrina fascists* II, 13: "The fascist State is a will to power and dominion" (una volunta di potenza e d'emperio). It is the tradition of ancient Rome which is appealed to here. Cf. A. MENZEL, *Der Staatsgedanke des Faschismus* (Leipzig und Wien, 1935) p.61. Cf. also pp.83 ff. *op.cit.*

2 Compare MUSSOLINI's statement in the article quoted from the *Enciclopedia Italiana:* "It is not the nation that creates the State, as was asserted in the naturalistic doctrine of the 19th century. But the nation is created by the State which only gives the people the consciousness of its own moral unity, a will, and therefore its real existence." The German national-socialist doctrine of the nation as "a community of blood," as a "racial community" was unconditionally rejected by MUSSOLINI. Cf. MENZEL *op.cit.* pp.74-75.

3 Cf., *e.g.*, WALZER HAMEL: *Volkseinheit und Nationalitätenstaat*, in Zeitschr. f. d. ges. Staatswissenschaft, Bnd. 95, 4e Heft, (1935), p.587.

4 Cf. MUSSOLINI's pronouncement at Naples in October 1922: "We have created a myth; a myth is a belief, a noble enthusiasm; it need not be a reality; it is an impulse and a hope, faith and courage. Our myth is the nation, the great nation, which we want to make into a concrete reality." Cf. A. MENZEL, *op.cit.* p.15-16. Cf. also GIULIANO BALBINO: *L'idea etica del fascismo* (in Gerarchia 1932, XI, p.949).

5 *Wesen des Staatsgebietes* (1933) p.231 If. Cf. also his treatise cited above.

strife, or if it lacks sufficient economical means to assert its power. But all this only proves what we have pointed out from the beginning, viz. that the typical foundational function in the structure of the State is not selfsufficient. It does not imply that the State is not typically *founded* in the monopolistic organization of the power of the sword over a territorial cultural sphere.

### The fundamental error of considering all different forms of power intrinsically equivalent components of the power of the State

For a real insight into the individuality-structure of the State it is essential to guard against the view which emphasizes the all-sidedness of political power and treats all its components alike. The fallacy of this opinion does not lie in the recognition that in a way State-power is all-sided. For as regards *its historical aspect,* the State is not *merely* the organized power of the sword over a particular territory. If the State did not have at its disposal typical economical, moral, pisteutic and other forms of power,[1] it would even be *impossible* to form a military organization. But this is not the point at issue. None of the other forms of power is in itself typical of *the State*. The monopolistic organization of the power of the sword is the only typical form which *is not found as a foundational function* in any of the other differentiated societal structures. The other forms of power, insofar as they are really *internal* forms of State-power, are themselves only intelligible from the structural principle of the body politic, which implies a monopolistic military organization as its typical foundational function. They may also belong to the *variability-types* of the State, which originate from enkaptic interweavings with other societal structures.

To give an example: if there are powerful industries, large-scale agricultural undertakings, worldwide shipping organizations, *etc.,* within its territory, the power of the State is closely bound up with the prosperity of these non-political organizations. But this does not mean that the economic forms of power of these organizations, which in modern times are for a good deal of an *international* character, are internal constituents of the power of the State.

There may be an open antagonism between the power of the State and that of industry or commerce, if the latter abuse their means for political aims contrary to "national interests." A State whose organized military power is weak will never be a *powerful State,* though having large economic means of power, a very rich soil, a flourishing science and art within its territory. If the levelling schema of the whole and its parts is applied to the relation between the power of the State and the other structures of power within its territory, the resulting conclusions will always be in conflict with reality. They misinterpret the individuality-structures of reality. On this error is based the mythological character of the idea of the totalitarian State. No matter how this idea is elaborated, it always implies that all the other individuality-structures of this power will retain their own essential character when they are made into internal con-

---

[1] These other forms of power are anticipatory forms of historical power, enclosed by the modal structure of the historical law-sphere, and having no original economic, moral, or faith modality. Cf. [NC] Vol.II, pp.7071.

stituents of the State's power. But all forms of power that really become internal elements of the power of the body politic must necessarily assume the internal individuality-structure of the latter. We have discovered that all mythology is a false interpretation of God's revelation in creaturely meaning. So also this political mythology rests on a false deification of the creaturely expression of God's omnipotence in the meaning-structure of the State's power.

...

### The invariable character of the foundational function in the structure of the State

The *original* character of the individuality-type implied in the foundational function of the State has thus been established. We will now engage in a more detailed analysis of the monopolistic organization of the power of the sword over a territorial cultural area, as the typical foundational function in the structure of the body politic. In its transcendental character this foundational function cannot be eliminated from the structural principle which makes all variable real life of the State only possible and is itself invariable, constant, in the cosmic order of time. No "idealistic" theory has been able to reason away this structural foundation of every real State. The "metaphysical essence" of the body politic could be sought in the "idea of justice," or in the idea of a perfect community, but the basic function of the historical power of the body politic could not be ignored consistently.

This structural foundation is essential in every positive historical form in which the State has manifested itself in the course of time: in the Greek *polis* and in the Roman world-empire, as well as in the Carolingian State and the Italian city-States of Renaissance times; in the absolute French monarchy that developed under the *"ançient régime"* after the annihilation of the political power of the "estates," as well as in the constitutional State after the French Revolution; in the modern parliamentary democracies, as well as in the recent form of the totalitarian dictatorial States. It is quite true that the foundational military organization of power may have been weakened and endangered by military organizations of certain groups or parties within the State's territory. This may even justify the question whether in such a condition we had not better speak of a revolutionary chaos instead of a real body politic. It is also possible that a young State has not yet completely succeeded in monopolizing the organized power of the sword within its territory, without giving up its claim to this monopoly. But, as we have repeatedly emphasized, our discussion is concerned with *a normative structural function* implying a *task,* a *vocation* for the internal organization of the State's power.[1] This vocation can be fulfilled in a better or a worse way. It may be that in a certain part of its territory the body politic has actually monopolized the organized military power, and that outside of this area the State is only "a name." But all these really variable situations do not detract from the universal validity of the normative structural principle of the State, which implies the territorial monopolistic organization of military power as its typical foundational function. If in a well-ordered

---

1  Cf. [NC] Vol.II, pp.246 ff.

body politic a revolution breaks out, this state of affairs is put to the test; and it is proved that the structural relation mentioned cannot at all be altered by human arbitrariness. Such a revolution may be prepared by theoretical and practical political propaganda, by exerting a systematic influence on "national conviction." But as soon as the revolutionary leaders want to take the government in their own hands, they must start with mastering the organized military apparatus either with sanguinary or with bloodless means.

> In his famous article in the *Enciclopedia Italiana* on the *Doctrina fascista* MUSSOLINI seemed to represent the fascist idea of State-power as an idea of *moral* authority, in which the territorial military organization would not at all have a typical foundational position.[1] But this statement was concerned with international relations of power. Contrary to it there are many others in which the peculiar position of organized military power in the structure of the State is fully recognized, and even absolutized.[2] The fascist revolution culminated in the historical march on Rome. This was an illustration of our exposition of the foundational place which the monopolistic organization of military power over a territory occupies in the structure of the State.

A truly political revolution which pulls down the existent government of a body politic, is radically different from a revolution which is typically founded in other historical structures of power and typically guided and directed by another leading function than that of the body politic. There are revolutions in science, in art, in the Church, *etc.*, which as such do not have any *political* character.

### The structural subject-object relation in the monopolistic organization of military power over a territorial cultural area

According to its individuality-structure this monopolistic organization of the power of the sword is not merely a *technical apparatus*. The foundational structural function of the State displays that typical subject-object relation which we already discovered when discussing the thing-structure of reality. It is true, the structural foundation of the State comprises an *objective* apparatus of military arms, buildings, aircraft, airports, *etc.* But this military apparatus, as a historical object, is only meaningful in connection with an organized

---

1 *Dottrina 11,13*: 'According to fascist theory, power is not a territorial, military or mercantile concept, but a moral and spiritual idea. It is quite well possible to imagine the working of a power exercised by one nation over another without the necessity of conquering even a quarter of a square mile of foreign territory' (quoted by A. MENZEL, *Der Staatsgedanke des Faschismus*, 1935, p.61). Indeed, such "influence of power" can be imagined. Recall, *e.g.*, the influence of cultural power that vanquished Hellas had on Rome! It may be doubted if MUSSOLINI would have been satisfied with such a *typically non-political* power for the "Italian nation." In addition it can be imagined that a mighty State controls its weak neighbours simply by the dread of its military power. But this possibility does not fit to the intention of MUSSOLINI's statement.

2 Cf. the Duce's essay: *My Thought on Militarism* (1934, quoted by MENZEL, *op.cit.* p.62): "The doom of a nation lacking a military spirit is sealed. For in the last instance it is war that is decisive in the relations between States. In my definition war is the supreme court of justice of the nations." Cf. also MENZEL, p.70.

army or police force. Only subjective military bearers of power can actualize this objective apparatus: without them it remains "dead material." As soon as we consider the organized military power of the State according to this subjective point of view, it is immediately evident how insufficient is a merely functionalistic technical conception. And also, how little this organized power can be *enclosed within*[1] in the historical law-sphere. Military rules of discipline, rigid military forms of organization appear to be powerless in an army or police-force in which a revolutionary mentality has undermined the sense that the authority of the present government is *legitimate*.[2]

It is evident here that the military organization of State power displays an opened, *anticipatory structure* that cannot be explained in terms of *merely* armed control.

All the same, this organization appeared to be an *original* historical type of individuality. The structural subject-object relation in the foundational function of the State is indeed very complicated. It also comprises the relation between the organized military power and the territorial cultural area of the body politic. From a modal historical standpoint this cultural area is to be viewed only as an object of the formative power of the State. From a structural viewpoint this historical aspect of the State-territory can never be conceived apart from the leading juridical function of this societal institution. But this necessary structural relation between the foundational and the leading function is no reason to ignore the peculiar modal meaning of the foundational function. *Military* organization of power in its historical modality is not of a *juridical* character. For this reason the area of the State's military power, as the object of the subjective formation of military control, cannot be grasped in a *modal juridical* sense.

...

## The levelling constructive schema of the whole and its parts confronted with the fourfold use of a fruitful idea of totality

Once the typical foundational function of the State has been theoretically pushed into the background, the entire individuality-structure of this societal institution will be eliminated. Then there seems to be no alternative for an "organic theory" but to construe the relationship between the body politic and the other societal structures according to the metaphysical schema of the whole and its parts. The remarkable and dangerous feature of an idea of totality, oriented to a constructive metaphysical principle of a perfect community like that found in ARTSTOTLE, is the indeterminateness of its meaning.[3] For it has not been oriented to the individuality-structures of human societal life.

---

1  *Editorial note* (DFMS): the original text reads: "*shut up.*"
2  There are good observations on this point in E. BRUNNER, *Das Gebot and die Ordnungen* (1932), pp.433 ff.
3  [NC] Vol.III, pp.201 ff.

Up to now we have found three different kinds of correct and fruitful use of the Idea of totality:[1]
1. in the Prolegomena, as the transcendental Idea of meaning-totality;
2. in the general theory of the modal spheres, as the Idea of the totality of structural moments in a meaning-modus;
3. in the theory of the individuality-structures of reality, as the idea of the whole of a thing or occurrence, or that of the whole of a particular relationship of human social life.

In this threefold use the Idea always remained oriented to a divine world-order which did not originate in "reason," but limited and determined reason itself. In the constructive levelling abuse of this Idea, it loses its essential structural character and the delimitation of its meaning.

Later on we shall discover a fourth use of the totality-Idea, viz. as *the Idea of the integration of human societal relations*. Then we can do justice to the moment of truth in the totality-Idea of the universalistic theories. At the same time, however, we shall find that the Idea of totality in this fourth application remains absolutely bound to that in the first, second and third uses. Apart from these three it must lead to a fundamentally false construction of the mutual relations between the societal structures.

## THE TYPICAL LEADING FUNCTION OF THE STATE AND THE THEORY OF THE SO-CALLED 'PURPOSES' OF THE BODY POLITIC

We will now examine the typical leading function of the State's structure in its indissoluble coherence with the foundational function analyzed above.

At the outset we warned against identifying the leading or qualifying structural function of a thing with the purposes it is to serve. We have repeated this warning with reference to the inner structure of natural communities. Similarly, the leading or qualifying function of an organized human community should not be misinterpreted as the end or ends that human beings try to reach in this relationship by means of their organized endeavours. This warning is especially to the point in the case of the typical leading function in the structure of the State.

### *The theories of the "purposes of the State" bear no reference to the internal structural principle of the body politic*

The theory of the purpose of the State is as old as political philosophy. It is burdened with the great diversity of meanings implied in the word "purpose," which is used now in a metaphysical-realistic, now in a subjectivistic-nominalistic sense, now in an absolute, then in a relative way. In immanence-philosophy the theory of the purpose of the body politic sometimes contained an *a priori* rational construction, serving to justify the State, and thus assumed

---
[1] The reader should remember that the *Idea* of totality is to be sharply distinguished from the modal *concept* of totality. The latter is merely a provisional resting-point for thought and only embraces the *restrictive* structure of a meaning-modus; it is transcendentally dependent on the *Idea* of totality.

an explicit *biological* character.

Realistic scholasticism used this theory to prove that the institutional Church is of a higher value than the State. The Humanistic doctrine of natural law and that of *"Vernunftrecht,"* in their subjectivistic-teleological constructions of the body politic, made the latter into a mere instrument in the service of the individual or into that of a national cultural community. Then the "purpose of the State" was conceived in the sense of the classical liberal idea of the law-State[1] (LOCKE, KANT, v. HUMBOLDT) or in the eudaemonistic sense of the "welfare State" (the police-State of CHR. WOLFF and his pupil JUSTI). Or again in the idealistic sense of a culture-State (FICHTE is his last phase).[2] But this teleology never had any inner relation to the real *structural principle* of this societal institution. From a historical standpoint the different theories of the subjective "purpose of the State" propounded in the Humanistic doctrines of natural law prove to be only the expression of a political tendency at the time of their inception. This explains why they became untenable as soon as the historical situation changed. Hence the futility of every attempt to grasp the intrinsic structural limits to the task of the State in such a teleological way.

### *The old liberal theory of the law-State as a theory of the purpose of the body politic*

We shall once more consider the Humanistic theory of the law-State.[3]

In its first stage, viz. the classical natural-law stage (LOCKE, KANT, VON HUMBOLT), this theory aimed at limiting the "purpose of the body politic" construed in the social contract. The State was supposed to have no other aim than the organized protection of the "innate absolute human rights" of all its citizens to freedom, property and life. It should not interfere with the non-political society which by the liberal economic theory was viewed under an exclusively economical aspect and sharply distinguished from the body politic. Thus this theory was the expression of the old-liberal programme of non-interference (*"laisser faire, laisser passer"*). But its starting-point was an individualist-nominalistic view of reality and could not but eliminate the structural leading function of the State-institution. "Law" itself was conceived in the individualistic natural-law sense of "innate subjective rights" and supposed to be a "purpose" lying outside of the State. In an earlier context we called LOCKE's "law-State" a limited liability company continuing the "state of nature" under the protection of governmental authority.[4]

In KANT's idea of the law-State, public law and civil law are materially identified. Civil law "guarantees the external 'mine' and 'dine' by means of State-

---

1  The term law-State is used here in the sense of the German term *"Rechtsstaat,"* which is not to be adequately rendered by "rule of law."

2  FICHTE defended his idea of a culture-State in his *Staatslehre* (1813).

3  My view of the development of this theory has been amply elaborated in the standard work of Prof. Dr. J.P.A. MEKKES, *Proeve eener critische Beschouwing [van de ontiwkkeling] der Humanistische Rechtsstaatstheorieen* (Utrecht-Rotterdam, 1940), 752 pp.

4  [NC] Vol.I, part.II, p.318.

laws."¹ KANT's "concept of law" (in his way of thought it should be called his normative *Idea* of law) is nothing but an *a priori* idea of civil private law, the principle of civil-legal coexistence: "Law is the totality of the conditions under which the arbitrary will of one individual with the arbitrary will of another can be united according to a general law of freedom."²

This idea was further defined, by applying THOMASIUS' criterion of law as a *coercive* regulation, as "the possibility of a mutual universal constraint which is in agreement with everybody's freedom according to general rules."³

The classical liberalistic idea of the law-State finds its pregnant expression in KANT's pronouncement on the contents of public law: "The latter does not contain any more or any other duties of human beings to one another than can be thought of in the former (*i.e.* in the natural state of private law); the matter of private law is exactly the same in both. The rules of the latter are therefore only concerned with the legal form of its union (constitution), with respect to which these rules must necessarily be considered as public."⁴

In the "*trias politica*"⁵ postulated by this idea of the State, in which according to MONTESQUIEU's prescription, the legislative, the executive, and the judiciary powers ought to be kept strictly apart and equilibrated, the "executive authority" is merely an alien element ("*Fremdkorper*"). There is no room for an "administrative authority" with an independent positive task in this civil-law idea of the body politic. The State has become a *form* ("*Verfassung*") for private juridical life.

The only thing in this idea of the law-State reminiscent of the internal structure of the body politic is the *coercive* character of the legal order. It has been conceived in an undefined "general concept" of "coercion," and is connected with the idea of freedom, as the supposed normative *essence* of justice, in a

---

1  *Metaphysik der Sitten, 1er Teil* (W.W. Grosh. Wilhelm Ernst Ausg. V), p.425.
2  *Op.cit.* p.335: "Recht ist der Inbegriff der Bedingungen, unter welchen die Willkür des Einen mit der Willkur des Andern nach einem allgemeinen Gesetze der Freiheit zusammen vereinigt werden kann."
3  *Op.cit.* p.337: ..."die Möglichkeit eines mit jedermans Freiheit nach allgemeinen Gesetzen zusammenstimmenden durchgängigen wechselseitigen Zwanges."
4  *Op.cit.* pp.425-426: "Dieses enthalt nicht mehr, oder andere Pflichten der Menschen unter sich als in jenem (*i.e.* in dem Zustand des Privatrechts) gedacht werden konnen; die Materie des Privatrechts ist eben dieselve in beiden. Die Gesetze des letzteren betreffen also nur die rechtliche Form ihres Beisammenseins (Verfassung), in Ansehung deren diese Gesetze notwendig als öffentlich gedacht werden müssen." Compare also the extremely vague definition of public law in § 43 (p.431) *op.cit.*: "Der Inbegriff der Gesetze, die einer allgemeinen Bekantmachung bedurfen um einen rechtlichen Zustand hervorzubringen, ist das *öffentliche Recht*. Dieses ist also ein System vom Gesetzen für ein Volk, d.i. eine Menge von Menschen, oder für eine Menge van Völkern, die im wechselseitigen Einflusse gegen einander stehend, des rechtlichen Zustandes unter einem sie vereinigenden Willen, einer *Verfassung* (constitutio) bedürfen, um dessen, was Rechtens ist, teilhaftig zu werden." [The totality of the rules that require general publication in order to create a legal order, is *public law*. This is, therefore, a system of rules for a nation, *i.e.* a multitude of people, or for a multitude of nations who mutually influence each other and are in need of an organization (constitution) under one will that unites them, if they are to obtain that which is law.]
5  *Op.cit.* pp.433 ff.

characteristic logicistic-dialectical way: Legal *coercion is* the negation of a negation of freedom (injustice), according to general rules, and according to KANT it is thus consonant with freedom.

It is important to note that KANT thinks he must restrict this civil law idea of the law-State to the *internal* relations of the latter. In the *external* relations to other States he conceives of the body politic only as a "power," as a "potentate."[1] In KANT's definition of the State, as the "union of a multitude of people under legal rules,"[2] the foundational function has been ignored, almost on purpose. He apparently derived this definition from CICERO. But even KANT's critical freedom-idealism could not carry this disregard through consistently.

### The theory of the law-State in its second phase as the theory of the merely formal limitation of the purposes of the State. The formalistic conception of administrative jurisdiction

In its second phase (STAHL, OTTO BAHR, RUDOLPH GNEIST) the theory of the law-State was not really a theory of the purpose of the body politic any longer. It assumed a formalistic character: the old liberal idea of the law-State was transformed into that of the rule of statute law. Law, in the sense of a civil legal order protecting the subjective innate rights of man, was no longer considered to be the *purpose* of the body politic. Instead, the idea of the law-State was now related to a public administrative legal order as a *formal limit* to which the magistrature would have to be bound in its administrative activities, when promoting cultural and welfare purposes. This formal legal limitation was required in the interest of the legal security of the citizens. This "legal restriction" of the "executive authority" was found by subordinating the administrative organs to legislation. The statute law was to protect the citizens from administrative arbitrariness. In this sense the modern idea of the law-State was formulated by FR. JULIUS STAHL in his statement: "The State should be a law-State... It should accurately determine the roads and boundaries of its activity as well as the free spheres of its citizens in a legal way... and it should not realize the ethical ideas any further than insofar as they belong to the legal sphere. The concept of the law-State is not that the body politic only maintains the legal order without any administrative purposes, or accords only complete protection to the rights of individuals; it does not mean the aim of the State but

---

[1] *Metaph. der Sitten* (the edition cited), p.431. Cf. also FR. DARMSTAEDTER: *Die Grenzen der Wirksamkeit des Rechtsstaates* (Heidelberg, 1930), p.2. HEINRICH RICKERT's pronouncement in his *Kant als Philosoph der modernen Kultur* (Tübingen 1924), p.113, that KANT would have held the view "the State is power," is to be restricted to the international relationshics as long as no international jurisdiction has been instituted. Besides, KANT could only conceive of power in an *empirical naturalistic* sense.

[2] *Metaph. d. S.* (the edition cited), p.433.

only the mode and character of realizing its political ends."[1] In itself this utterance seems to be quite acceptable. But in the context of STAHL's view of law it implied that public administrative law was depreciated to a merely formal law and opposed to (civil) *material* law in a dualistic way. According to STAHL the principles of *material law* are to be found in the Decalogue, and the subjective private rights are in principle grounded in the latter.

It is evident that in this conception of the law-State the legal order is connected with the power of the body politic only in an *external, formal* way. STAHL, and all the adherents of this idea of the law-State, look upon administrative law only as a formal limitation ("*Schranke*") within which the government can operate free of material legal principles when pursuing the "cultural and welfare purposes."

The non-juridical "purposes of the State" are not given any internal structural delimitation, if their administrative realization is only bound to the formal limits of legislation. This formalistic conception of public law is closely connected with the equally formalistic, and essentially civil juridical view of *administrative judicature,* represented as a requirement of the modern constitutional State by the Hessian jurist OTTO BAHR[2] and RUDOLPH GNEIST.[3]

Even at the present time it is customary to distinguish between *legal questions* and *utility questions* in the theory of administrative judicature. The *merely formally conceived legal questions* are subjected to the decision of the administrative judge; but the material, internal legal questions are not, because the latter are qualified as "questions of utility." This is really a consequence of the formal idea of the law-State, and shows a lack of a really structural conception of the internal law of the body politic. We shall recur to this point in a later context.

In its second phase the theory of the law-State is the expression of a political tendency that has radically broken with the old-liberal programme of political non-interference with the free (non-political) society. The "executive" is here subjected to the formal limits set by the legislature as far as the State's administrative task is concerned. This task is supposed to be the peculiar domain in which the body politic has to promote the prosperity and the "culture" of the national community.

---

1 FR. JULIUS STAHL, *Philosophie des Rechts nach geschichtlicher Ansicht* (3e Aufl.) End. II, I, pp.137-138: "Der Staat soll Rechtsstaat sein... Er soll die Bahnen und Grenzen seiner Wirksamkeit wie die freie Sphäre seiner Burger in der Weise des Rechts genau bestimmen... und soll die sittlichen Ideen von staatswegen nicht weiter verwirklichen als es der Rechtsphäre angehört. Dies ist der Begriff des Rechtsstaates, nicht etwa dass der Staat bloss die Rechtsordnung handhabe ohne administrative Zwecke, oder vollends bloss die Rechte der Einzelnen schütze, er bedeutet nicht Ziel des Staates sondern nur Art und Charakter, dieselben zu verwirklichen."

2 O. BAHR, *Der Rechtsstaat*, p.134, explicitly demands that "the power of the government... in its application..., just like private rights, shall be subordinate to the law" ("die Regierungsgewalt... in ihrer Betätigung... *gleich den Privatrechten unter* dem Rechte stehen soll").

3 R. GNEIST, *Der Rechtsstaat.*

# POLITICAL PHILOSOPHY

*The third phase in the development of the theory of the law-State. The uselessness of any attempt to indicate fundamental external limits to the State's task by the construction of limited subjective purposes of the body politic*

The extreme denaturing of the idea of the law-State is seen in its *third stage of development*. Then it no longer purports to be a political idea of the legal delimitation of the State's task but is viewed to be nothing but a logical consequence of methodical purity in the general theory of the body politic. This conception has found expression in the theory of KELSEN and his school. In this theory State and law are identified at the expense of the entire content of both the idea of the State and that of law.

In the logicist formalism of this school even the "dictatorial absolutist State" formally becomes a "law-State," in which the executive has only gained absolute priority over the legislature. For, according to KELSEN, every State must be "logically" conceived as "law."[1] Thus this concept of the law-State also embraces the totalitarian absolutist State and thereby loses any material normative meaning.

Indeed, even the national socialist and fascist power-States laid claim to the qualification of true or *material law-States*. Yet their ideology did not recognize any material juridical limits to the competence of the authority of the body politic.[2]

This fact in itself is important insofar as it shows that these political ideologies could not completely ignore the structural principle of the body politic, notwithstanding their overstraining the idea of power. For in this structural principle the juridical function has indeed the typical leading role.

Another fact, too, is evident, viz. how little the traditional idea of the law-State was oriented to the invariable internal structure of the latter. The classical individualistic liberal idea of the body politic ignored the typical public communal law of the State in the sphere of public administration, but claimed the monopoly of being "an idea of the law-State." The same privilege was claimed by the formal idea of the law-State with its formalistic conception of public law. But we fail to see what entitled these views to such an exclusive claim. Also the Italian fascist State formally bound its organs to the prevailing legal norms and allowed for a certain administrative judicature. This State, just like the German "third Empire" *(Dritte Reich)*, pretended to realize a material, universalistic conception of law, in contradistinction to the formalistic and individualistic legal idea.

---

1  Cf. my *De Crisis in de Humanistiche Staatsleer*, p.45 and KELSEN's statement quoted there.

2  Cf. for the fascist ideology of the *stato giuridico* (law-State) MENZEL, pp.73 ff., GIUSEPPE LO VERDE, *Die Lehre vom Staat im neuen Italien* (Berlin 1934) pp.54 ff. and S. PANUNZIO, *Allgemeine Theorie des fascistischen Staates* (Berlin und Leipzig, 1934) pp.78 ff. For the German national-socialist ideology of the law-State C. KOELLREUTER, *Deutsches Verfassungsrecht*, p.12, CARI. SCHMIDT, *Nationalsozialismus und Rechtsstaat* (J.W. 1934, 63 Jg., Heft 12/13) and G. HAVESTADT, *Der Staat und die nationale Gesamtordnung* (Arch. d. öff. R., N.F. 27 Bnd., I Heft, 1936, pp.76 ff.

From the outset the old liberal theory of the law-State lacked the insight into the typical internal structure of the legal function as the leading function of the body politic. This explains why it could not really stem the rising tide of the idea of the totalitarian State. For the historical development made fresh demands on public life incompatible with the earlier political conceptions of the State's purposes.

The attempt to curtail political absolutism by means of the construction of restricted "purposes of the State" was doomed to failure. The political ideas about the external extent of the State's task are necessarily dependent on historical development. They should not be confounded with the invariable normative structural principle of the body politic.[1]

KELSEN must undeniably be credited with having detected this weak spot in the anti-absolutist theory of the restricted "purposes of the State." He opposed the introduction of "political postulates" in the general theory of the State. But his own "normological" theory resulted in the theoretical negation of both State and law.

The question what concrete subjective purposes a body politic has to realize at different times and in different places, presupposes the internal structure of the State as such. This is the first insight to be gained if we want to grasp the internal leading function of this societal institution. A State cannot serve any "purposes" if it does not *exist as such*. And it can have no real existence except within the cadre of its *internal structural principle* determining its essential character.

...

### The typical leading function of the State in its indissoluble coherence with its foundational function

As soon as the confusing totalitarian identification of the State and the whole of human society is abandoned and the nature of the body politic as a *differentiated republic* is acknowledged, the tracing of its typical leading function becomes indispensable.

This typical leading function as a structural qualification of the State-institution is only to be found in the juridical law-sphere.

---

[1] This confusion also occurs in G. JELLINEK, *Allgemeine Staatslehre* (3e Aufl. 1919), pp.235 ff. He posits that only such a definition which takes the State's purposes into account, can offer a well-defined criterion to distinguish the body politic from other societal structures (*e.g.*, the Church). This thesis is closely connected with his subjectivistic individualistic conception of an organized community as a "purposive unity" (*Zweckeinheit*) in a socio-psychological sense. Cf. *op.cit.* p.179: "Eine Vielheit von Menschen wird für unser Bewusstsein geeinigt wenn sie durch konstante, innerlichkoharente Zwecke mit einander vereinigt sind." [To our consciousness a plurality of people are united when they are combined by constant, internally cohering purposes]. Therefore in his opinion the sociological theory of the State should point out 'those purposes by means of which the multiplicity of people united in the State appear to us as a unity' (*op.cit.* p.234). Meanwhile JELLINEK has not succeeded in showing an inner coherence between the different political aims of the modern State so that they are to be conceived as a unity.

It is in vain to seek for another qualifying aspect. That a real body politic cannot be *qualified* by its territorial military power-formation must be evident as soon as we consider that, as a *res publica,* it is always in need of the subordination of its armed force to the civil government in order to guarantee that *stability* of its public legal order which is characteristic of a State. A temporary delegation of the governmental authority to a military commander has in the nature of the case an exceptional character. It is an emergency measure to which a body politic has only recourse in times of war or revolutionary disorder. But in its internal structure the monopolistic military organization is always subservient to a stable territorial public legal order, which also in international law is the ultimate criterion of the existence of a State. This order is only *founded* in a monopolistic organization of armed force.

KELSEN has convincingly shown that every attempt of a naturalist or cultural-scientific sociology to gain a concept of the State apart from the normative legal viewpoint, is doomed to fail. His erroneous identification of the body politic with a system of legal norms can only be explained by the fact that the juridical aspect has indeed a qualifying position in the structural principle of this organized community. This is precisely the difference between the State and all differentiated communities of a non-political character. It is true that the latter also have an internal legal sphere. But they are never *qualified* by this internal juridical function.

A real State cannot find its qualifying function in any other than the juridical aspect, and without this leading function it would degenerate into an organized military gang of robbers, because of its very foundation in armed force.

This is not merely a *specific* difference, but it distinguishes the body politic *radically* from the non-juridically qualified organized communities, such as a Church, an industrial community, a family, a school, a club, *etc.* But the State's qualifying function can only be grasped in its structural coherence with its typical foundational function. The indissoluble, typical-internal structural coherence between "right and might" in the State-relationship is first of all expressed in the *structure of its authority*.

In contradistinction to this structure in all non-political communal relationships, authority in the State, according to its inner nature, is *governmental authority* over subjects *enforced by the strong arm*.[1]

The government does not carry the sword in vain. It has been invested with the power of the sword, and as soon as the sword slips out of its hands, it is no longer a government. But according to the structure of its divine office this power is internally directed to the structural guidance by that typical legal communal function whose type of individuality is *founded* in this sword-control. All internal communal law of the State-institution in a structural sense is public territorial law imposing itself with governmental legal authority and maintained with the strong arm. Its sphere of competence will appear to find its internal limits in this structure itself.

---

1 Cf. on this KARL LARENZ, *Staatsphilosophie* (München und Berlin, 1933), p.177.

That is why GIERKE's elaborate discussion[1] of the *"Obrigheitsstaat"* in contrast with the *"Volksstaat,"* oriented to the "Germanic associational mind," is misleading, at least *terminologically,* and also *historically.* Every true State is essentially an *"Obrigkeitsstaat,"* according to the internal structure of its authority. But governmental authority is certainly not identical with some bureaucratic, centralistic and absolutist form of organization, excluding any active participation of popular organs in governmental affairs. MAURICE HAURIOU has rightly observed that the State-idea, which initially only influences a small elite undertaking its realization, has the natural tendency to *incorporate* itself in the whole of a people. What is really meant in GIERKE's contradistinction between *"Obrigkeitsstaat"* and *"Volksstaat"* is the contrast between the autocratic Roman imperium-idea and the democratic form of government. But the latter should not be brought in connection with the old Germanic and medieval Germanic associations which in their undifferentiated character were rather opposed to the State-idea.

*All* the pre-legal internal modal functions of the State should be guided by and directed to the territorial *public legal community* qualifying the body politic. A military usurper who does not perform the typical duties of the public legal office of the government can never be an organ of the *State*, but remains the leader of an organized gang of robbers. But on the other hand it must be emphatically repeated that the legal organization of the body politic, in its typical authoritative character, remains indissolubly founded in the historical organization of territorial military power. Apart from the latter, the internal public legal order of the State cannot display that *typical* juridical character which distinguishes it from all kinds of private law. It would be erroneous to suppose that this internal public law order lacks an inner *juridical* type of individuality and is only characterized by its external connection with the coercive apparatus of military power. We shall show in the sequel that it is rather characterized by typical legal principles. It was the disregard of the latter that led to the formalistic view of administrative jurisdiction mentioned above.

Only within the framework of its invariable structure can a *real* State-community be formed with an organized communal will. The "will of the State" is by no means a fictitious legal abstraction, but the real organized will of a communal whole. It is true that this will is *qualified* by the juridical relation between the government and its subjects, and *founded* in historical territorial military power. But it asserts itself in all the aspects of our social experience as an organized unity of volitional direction, realized in the *organized* actions of a societal whole. And it is fundamentally wrong to oppose this typical organization as a one-sided "mechanical" organization of governmental functions, to the people, as if the latter had an independent existence in opposition[2] to that of the government. After the definitive dissolution of the primitive popular and tribal organizations, no people of a differentiated cultural level exists otherwise than in a *public community*, by which it is indissolubly united

---

1 The Dutch text has *"overheidsgezag over onderdanen"* (German: *"Obrigkeitsgewalt über Untertäne"*). These pregnant terms are not to be rendered by adequate English words.

2 *Editorial note* (DFMS): the original text reads: "opposite."

with a government, as the bearer of authority. In the national State there does not exist *a people* apart from a government, and there is no *government* apart from a people. The people become a political unity only in the territorial organization of government and subjects. This truth must be strongly upheld against the romantic theory of the "people" as a mystic "natural organism."

The difficult question concerning the relation between a State, and a national community which is not identical with the political unity of a State's people, will demand our attention in a later context.

*The typical integrating character of the leading legal function in the structure of the State. The State's people as an integrated whole*

We have now arrived at the most critical point of our inquiry. The leading function in the structure of the State has proved to be a public legal relationship uniting government, people and territory into a politico-juridical whole. As the structural whole has priority to its constituents, it makes no sense to speak of the latter in terms of separate "elements" of the body politic. This is also to be kept in mind with respect to the leading juridical aspect of the State-institution. That the latter has nothing to do with a *particular aim* of the State has been shown above in our critical analysis of the old liberal idea of the law-State. A body politic cannot realize specific purposes unless it *exists as such*. And it cannot exist apart from its structural principle qualified by its leading function. This leading function lacks a *typical non-juridical qualification,* since the foundational function of power cannot supply this. In principle this implies the unique *universality* and *totality* of the internal legal community of the State, which is not found in any other societal structure.

The traditional universalistic theory of the State as the integral totality of all the other societal structures seems thus to be justified at least with regard to the *legal* organization of the body politic. In the internal structure of the State the *modal* juridical sphere-sovereignty does not seem to be individualized as a typical *structural juridical* sphere-sovereignty. But is the State, in its internal juridical sphere, really a juridical community with an unqualified coercive legal power, absorbing all the internal juridical relationships of a different radical and genotype, as its component parts?[1] This is impossible, since the individuality-structures of the non-juridically *qualified* legal relationships can never assume the structural character of public legal relationships inherent in the State. The relation between the typical universality of the internal public legal sphere of the State, and the qualified juridical spheres in non-political societal structures, cannot be conceived of in the schema of the whole and its parts.

The problem raised by the leading function of the State will perhaps be brought nearer to its solution if we remember that every body politic organizes a *people* within a territory into a typical, legally qualified, public community. The State's people is indeed the typical totality of all the citizens irrespective of their family-relations, their Church-membership or their philo-

---

1 *Editorial note* (DFMS): In other words, does the State encompass the internal legal order of non-political collectivities, such as the family, school, church, business, and so on.

sophical convictions, their trades or professions, class-distinctions, or their social standing. The State constitutes a typical *integrating* political unity in spite of any differences or divisions which its people display in other societal relationships.

How is this integration possible? The State cannot integrate these differences in profession or trade, ecclesiastical or philosophical trends, social classes, *etc.,* into the structure of a totalitarian professional or industrial organization, a totalitarian philosophical or Church community, or in the social structure of a totalitarian class. Nor can the State become an undifferentiated totality of all the "special" societal relationships within its territory. The integration of the citizens into the political unity of a people is in principle bound to the typical structure of the body politic, in which the leading function is that of a public legal community. This is an unparalleled, unique structural principle enabling the State to organize within its territory a truly universal legal communal bond transcending all non-juridically qualified legal societal relations. Neither internal ecclesiastical law, nor internal industrial law can have this typical *public juridical* integrating function, however large the number of the members of a Church or an industrial community may be. These legal spheres are limited by the typical particularity of their non-juridical qualification and lack the universally integrating character inherent in the internal public legal sphere of the State. In the territorial legal community of the body politic all the specifically qualified juridical interests should be harmonized in the sense of a truly public legal retribution, and integrated into "the public interest."

This implies that the principle of public interest must itself have a typical *juridical qualification which delimits its supra-arbitrary structural meaning.* It can never warrant an encroachment upon the internal sphere-sovereignty of non-political societal relationships. For the idea of an absolute competence of the State contradicts the modal meaning of the juridical aspect and is incompatible with the typical structural principle of the body politic. We shall recur to this point presently.

### The real structure of the internal public law. In the monistic legal theories this structure is ignored and an unjustified appeal is made to legal history

It is the principle of public interest which in its leading juridical aspect also gives a typical material legal meaning to the internal public law of the State. Wherever the State-structure, as such, expresses itself as a differentiated *res publica,* within the juridical aspect of human society, this public law appears. In unbreakable mutual coherence it embraces legal *organizational* and *behavior* norms. The former regulate the organization and competences of the different authoritative organs of the body politic; the latter regulate the public legal relations between the authoritative organs and the subjects. In spite of any enkaptic structural interlacements with civil private law, and with the non-political communal or inter-individual legal spheres, this public law retains its internal structure. True public communal law is never non-juridically *qualified,* although under the lead of the principle of public interest the legislator may pursue different political aims. Besides, the general principle of public interest will be differentiated in its material content by the different branches of the State's task, which varies with the historical development of a differentiated society.

> The functionalistic juridical theories do not know what to do with the concept of "public law" in its classical contradistinction to private law. This is not surprising since they do not take into consideration the internal structure of the State.

The view implied in these theories must result in the levelling of the individuality-structures. Such may be due to a formalist (logicistic) conception of law (KELSEN) or to a historicist-psychological view of the latter (KRABBE, V. IDSINGA). Insofar as such monistic theories make an appeal to medieval legal conditions,[1] to prove that the distinction between public and private law cannot be fundamental, we should be on our guard. It is necessary then to lay bare the structural-theoretical conditions of a really scientific historical inquiry into the human societal relationships, to unmask the *petitio principii* in this supposed "objective" historical demonstration. If the feudal medieval society lacked a fundamental distinction between public and private law, this can only be due to the fact that the undifferentiated condition of this society had not yet room for a real State. It can never prove that the distinction mentioned is not essential to the State as such.

It is not critical to seek for a fundamental distinction between public and private law in the Middle Ages without considering the preliminary question whether medieval society, as long as the feudal system prevailed, had any room for a real republican idea of governmental authority. In this connection we mention v. BELOW's studies of the "medieval German State." They are of special methodological importance, in as much as he has pointed out the erroneous absolutization of the economic-historical viewpoint in various monistic interpretations of the legal historical material. He has tried to deprive the monistic theory of one of its most cherished arguments, viz. the lack of a funda-

---

1 In addition an appeal is often made to the modern British legal system, which is supposed to lack a distinction between public and private law. But this is simply a misinterpretation of the "rule of (common) law" which could maintain itself in England almost until the end of the XIXth century. This "rule of law" had nothing to do with an elimination of the classical distinction between public and private law as such, which is as old as the State itself. It only meant that since the glorious Revolution there was no longer a specific royal administrative jurisdiction exempt from the courts of common law. DICEY praised this system and erroneously supposed that the French system of administrative jurisdiction had no other aim than to provide the organs of public administration with a privileged position. The truth was that in the long run the common law jurisdiction could not provide the citizens with a sufficient legal protection against administrative acts implying an undue encroachment upon their legal interests. The French *Conseil d'Etat* gave this protection in an exemplary way by applying typical public legal principles to the State's responsibility even when the latter might not be grounded on civil law rules which before 1912 were applied to unlawful acts of public administration by the *Cour de Cassation* (Cf. PAUL DUEZ, *La Responsabilité de la Puissance Publique*). And the British system of the "rule of common law" has since long been broken through by the introduction of a continually increasing administrative jurisdiction.

mental difference between public and private law in the Middle Ages.[1] Other German legal historians have followed him in this attempt.

But to my mind v. BELOW has not been able to free himself from the prejudice that the question as to whether we can speak of a real *State* in the Middle Ages, can be answered in a purely historical way. He also holds that we must not base our inquiry on structural theoretical insights into the essential character of the body politic.[2] This shows a lack of critical insight. Moreover, this historian has most certainly based his investigations on some structural theoretical insight into the nature of the State. This appears from the emphasis he has laid on the necessity of a juridical training of historians who want to examine the medieval political conditions.[3] In this context he could only mean that the legal historian should have an insight into the fundamental difference between public and private law inherent in the structure of the State. But this insight is not sufficient. The legal historian should also be aware of the danger of interpreting the medieval feudal system in terms of legal structural distinctions which only fit to a differentiated condition of human society. He should have a theoretical insight into the fundamental difference between undifferentiated and differentiated societal structures. How is the historian to gain such an insight from the changing historical facts if the latter are not included in supra-historical structures? These structures must first be clearly seen if the historian wants to interpret his legal material correctly.

From the historical viewpoint one should fight shy of a generalizing conception of the medieval political conditions. The political conditions of the late Middle Ages were very different from those of early and High medieval feudalism. And as to the Frankish kingdom there is a fundamental difference between the Merovingian *patrimonial regnum* and the Karolingian *State*, founded on the idea of the *res publica*. These differences are not duly considered by VON BELOW. Compare, for instance, his generalizing characterization of the public legal foundation of the Frankish empire (*Der deutsche Staat des Mittelalters*, pp.210 ff. with an appeal to WAITE, ROTH and SOHM) .

---

1 Cf. v. BELOW, *Der deutsche Staat des Mittelalters,* Bnd. I (2e Aufl. 1925). We would especially refer to the critical methodological remarks against straining the economical viewpoint: pp.75ff. Cf. also his: Die *Entstehung der deutschen Stadtgemeinde* (1889); *Der Ursprung der deutschen Stadtferfassung* (1892) and *Territorium und Stadt* (1900), especially pp.303 ff. Cf. also H. MITTEIS, *Lehnrecht and Staatsgewalt* (Weimar, 1933) pp.198 ff., pp.300, 321, 406, 516, 520, 575, etc.

2 Cf. *Der deutsche Staat des Mittelalters* (2e Aufl. 1925) p.xxv.

3 Cf. especially *op.cit.* p.84. Here v. BELOW blames NITSZCH for a fundamental lack of insight into the medieval political conditions on account of the fact that "notwithstanding his absorbing interest in the enquiry into the facts NITSZCH lacked that juridical intuition or training without which a description of constitutional history is simply unthinkable." ["dass ihm bei all seinem verzehrenden Interesse für die Erforschung der Realien die juristische Beanlagung oder Schulung gefehlt hat, ohne die nun einmal die Darstellung der Verfassungsgeschichte... undenkbar ist."]

## The real meaning of the absolutist idea of the State and the true idea of the law-State

A real public legal integration of a country and people is, therefore, only possible within the internal limits set by the structural principle of the State-institution itself. This integration can only be accomplished within the juridical limits set by this structural principle to the competence of the body politic, and with due regard to the internal sphere-sovereignty of the other societal structures. Every political theory denying these limits is in principle a theory of the "power-State," even though it masks its absolutization of the State's power by a law-State ideology.

In whatever shape the absolutist idea of the body politic is set forth, it does not recognize any intrinsic legal limits to the authority of the State. This idea implies an absorption of the entire juridical position of man by his position as citizen or as subject of the government.

If we cannot appeal to any law outside of the State, if the body politic has a so-called "*Kompetenz-Kompetenz*," i.e. a pseudo-juridical omnipotence, then the authority of the State has been theoretically deprived of any legal meaning and has in principle been turned into juridically *unlimited political power*. Neither a theoretical subjection of this power to some general principles of natural law, nor a theoretical construction of a so-called legal self-restriction of the State-power, can undo the harm implied in the initial absolutization inherent in the idea of sovereignty of the body politic, current since Bodin. But in the true idea of the law-State, the divine structural principle of the body politic limits the peculiar universality of the internal public law to a universality and sovereignty within its own sphere of competence. Every attempt on the part of an absolutist government to exceed the intrinsic boundaries of its legal power results in a despotism which undermines the very fundamentals of its authority. But even such a despotism can only occur within the structural principle of the body politic, which is beyond any human arbitrariness.

## The idea of "the public interest" and the internal limits set to it by the structural principle of the State

When we have gained an insight into the inner nature of the public legal communal sphere of the State, we can also find the *internal limits* to the idea of the "public interest" *as a guiding principle for the internal State-policy*. In the nature of the case this principle cannot be identical with its *leading juridical aspect*. But it is only the latter which can give to it its inner limitation as the material principle of public communal law.

The idea of the "*salus publica*" displays a genuine Protean character in political theory. It was made subservient to the ancient universalistic-organic theory of the State, to the doctrine of the "reasons of State," to WOLFF's natural law theory of the police-State, to HOBBES' and Rousseau's natural law construction of the Leviathan-State, but also to the classical liberal doctrine of the constitutional State (LOCKE and KANT), and to the modern totalitarian political theories.

For the sake of the public interest PLATO and FICHTE defended the withdrawal of the children from their parents and wanted their education to be entrusted to the body politic. With an appeal to the public interest PLATO wanted to abolish marriage and private property as far as the ruling classes of his ideal State were concerned. ARISTOTLE wanted education to be made uniform in "the public interest"; on the same ground Rousseau wished to destroy all the particular associations intervening between the State and the individual citizen. WOLFF desired the body politic to meddle with everything human and, at least for the Protestant Churches, he wanted the government to fix the confession. The idea of the "*salus publica*" was the hidden dynamite under the Humanistic natural law theories of HUGO GROTIUS and S. PUFENDORFF.[1] In CHR. WOLFF's doctrine of natural law this idea resulted in a frankly admitted antinomy with his theory of innate natural rights.[2] The slogan of the public interest was the instrument for the destruction of the most firmly established liberties because it lacked any juridical delimitation.

The terrible threat of Leviathan is audible in this word as long as it is used in a juridically unlimited sense. The universalistic political theories could conceive of the relation between the State and the non-political societal structures only in the schema of the whole and its parts. This is why they could not delimit the idea of "the public interest."

According to ARISTOTLE the State, as the autarchical "perfect community," has to supply its citizens any good they cannot obtain either individually or in the "lower communities." This is not an inner structural criterion of the legal limits of the public interest but only one for the external extent of the State's task. It is oriented to a metaphysical theory of the *purpose* of the State, and is entirely in accordance with the ancient totalitarian idea of the body politic. In this conception there is in principle no possibility of freedom outside of the State.

ROUSSEAU's idea of the "public interest" was only limited by the natural law principle of the equality of all the citizens before the statute law and consequently by the exclusion of any private privileges of individuals. This idea was to be expressed in the "general will" (la *'volonté générale'*); it did not imply any material legal restriction of competence of the legislator; it sanctioned the absolutist power of the State over all spheres of life, even over public worship.

CHR. WOLFF'S criterion of the *salus publica* is based on his eudaemonist[3] theory of natural law, and is identical with his conception of the purpose of the State embodied in the social contract. In his opinion the public interest consists in the *vitae sufficientia, tranquillitas et se-*

---

[1] Cf. my *In den Strijd om een Christelijke Staatkunde*, I, XV (A.R. Staatk. driemeand. orgaan, 1e jg.) pp.142 ff
[2] CHR. WOLFF, *Jus Naturae* VIII, 1, § 117; here he speaks of a real "*collisio legum*" between his principles of natural law and the basic principle of his theory of the State: "*Salus publica supreme lex esto.*" He cuts the Gordian knot with his construction of an emergency law of the State: "*Necessitas non subditur leg.*"
[3] *Editorial note* (DFMS): *Eudaemonism* represents an urge towards *happiness*.

*curitas*.[1] This view was oriented to the absolutist idea of the police-State that the "enlightened despots" in Prussia and Austria tried to realize.

As far as I know, KANT was the first Humanist philosopher who tried to give the idea of the *salus publica* an entirely new meaning, which was anti-absolutist and non-eudaemonistic. The eudaemonistic conception of the public interest was in conflict with KANT's practical idea of autonomy.

According to WOLFF, who is here in line with ARISTOTLE, the State should procure all the commodities its citizens need for their temporal well-being and perfection, insofar as the smaller communities of family and kinship cannot provide them. This was the only conception of the adage "*Salus publica supreme lex esto*" which was supposed to guarantee a rationally justified constitution. But KANT breaks with this eudaemonist conception. According to him the idea of the *salus publica* can have no other meaning than that of a constitutional principle containing the *a priori* juridical norms which ought to be realized as a duty prescribed by a categorical imperative. The contents of these juridical principles are found in KANT's conception of the law-State and its idea of the *trias politica*. We saw, however, that this idea of the law-State does not approach the internal structural limits to public law but is essentially an individualistic civil law idea. In KANT's conception the internal structure of the State is reduced to a mere organizational form for the creation, the maintenance, and the judicial application of private civil law (the organized form of the legislature, the police and the administration of justice).[2]

The idea of *salus publica* should be oriented to the structural principle of the State, else it will become the instrument of an unbridled State-absolutism, or the embodiment of an arbitrary conception of the external content of the State's task. In spite of all theoretical misconceptions of this principle it has a universally valid meaning, internally delimiting all real political activity of the State.

The *positive* contents of this principle, however, are dependent on an intricate complex of variable socio-cultural conditions.

---

1  *Jus Naturae* VIII, 1, §2.
2  *Met. Anfangsgründe der Rechtslehre* 2er Teil, 1er Abschnitt §49 in fine (Grossh. Wilhelm Ernst Ausg. V, p.439).

## The salus publica and distributive justice

In its qualifying juridical aspect the *public interest* implies the typical public legal measure of distributive justice which requires proportional distribution of public communal charges and public communal benefits in accordance with the bearing power and the merits of the subjects.[1] In his book *La Responsabilité de la Puissance Publique,* the French professor of constitutional law PAUL DUEZ has especially pointed to the significance of this public legal standard in the administrative jurisdiction of the French *Conseil d'Etat.* But it is of a universal import with respect to the whole internal public administration and administrative legislation. And as a legal principle of the public interest it clearly contradicts the erroneous opinion that administrative law is only a formal juridical framework for the pursuing of communal aims.

The *salus publica,* thus conceived, is a political integrating principle binding all the variable political maxims to a supra-arbitrary standard. It binds the entire activity of the State to the typical leading idea of public social justice in the territorial relations between government and subjects. Externally the task of the State cannot be delimited in a universally valid way, because the body politic, as a real organized community, functions in all the aspects of temporal reality. In principle, it is impossible even to exclude the State from the spheres of morality and faith. The State may promote the interests of science and the fine arts,[2] education, public health, trade, agriculture and industry, popular morality, and so on. But every governmental interference with the life of the nation is subject to the inner vital law of the body politic, implied in its structural principle. This vital law delimits the State's task of integration according to the political criterion of the "public interest," bound to the principle of sphere-sovereignty of the individuality-structures of human society.

The internal political activity of the State should always be guided by the idea of public social justice. It requires the harmonizing of all the interests obtaining within a national territory, insofar as they are enkaptically interwoven with the requirements of the body politic as a whole. This harmonizing process should consist in weighing all the interests against each other in a retributive sense, based on a recognition of the sphere-sovereignty of the various societal relationships.

---

1 KANT, and the Humanistic teachers of natural law before him, did not understand the original Aristotelian sense of the idea of distributive justice. This idea originally bore on the internal communal law of the State, and not on private civil juridical relations as intended in KANT's idea of law as a normative principle of juridical coexistence. We have shown in an earlier context that even the Aristotelian conception of commutative justice is not to be understood in an individualistic sense. KANT, however, understands by *iustitia distributive* or *"austeilende Gerechtigkeit"* only such justice as is administered by a civil judge, as an impartial instance created by the "general will" for deciding private legal disputes. Cf. *Met. Anfangsgründe,* I §§ 39 and 41.

2 Remember that in case the modern State gives financial support, this is done with revenues from taxation levied from its citizens by means of governmental coercion. Statesupport is therefore something quite different from that given by a private association for the promotion of sciences or the fine arts, because in associations the members give support out of their own free will.

To give a concrete example, we will consider the administrative juridical regulation of the many-sided concern of public health. This is a real concern of the public legal sphere of the State which, as such, is not qualified by a non-juridical aspect. The particularity of the subject matter of this administrative legal regulation is its concern with the bio-social structural aspect of the national community. Nevertheless, the regulation itself ought to be guided by the public legal principle inherent in the "public interest."

No doubt such a positive regulation is intended to serve a particular political purpose, viz. the improvement of public health. This purpose in itself does not differ from the aims of private societies for the improvement of national health. But this part of administrative law, as well as all the relevant executive measures taken by the organs of the State, has an internal, public juridical qualification. The internal structure of administrative law makes it obligatory on the government always to weigh the various private legal interests carefully against each other, and against the "public interest," in a retributive sense. These private interests must be harmonized and integrated in the public juridical interest. This is not required in the case of private societies for the promotion of public health, whose structure has a non-juridical qualification, and which are not founded in military power.

## *The civil law-sphere of the State*

The internal public law-sphere of the State has its typical correlate in the sphere of civil law as a private *common law* (*ius commune*). Every communal legal sphere is correlated with inter-individual legal relationships. But in addition to its correlation with the typical international relations of a public law character, the public communal law-sphere of the State has a *typical* correlate in an inter-individual legal sphere which is unbreakably bound to the structure of the body politic.

It is true that private common law does not immediately develop within the framework of the State so long as the undifferentiated societal relationships have not yet been completely conquered. The Carlovingian State did not succeed in replacing the ancient barbarian tribal laws by a common private legal order. This body politic lacked stability, and before Charlemagne's organization of the public administration could be followed by the development of a private common civil law, the republican empire collapsed.

The Roman republic started with an elevation of the primitive ancient intergentilitial law of the Quiritian tribes to a civil law bound to Roman citizenship. The *lex duodecim tabularum* was nothing but a description of old customary rules and was on the same primitive level as the barbarian *lex Salica* described under the reign of the Merovingian king CHLODOVECH.

It was only under the influence of the *ius gentium* that the idea of a *common private law* developed. Initially this *ius gentium* did not exceed the boundaries of a law containing the common ingredients in the legal customs of the old Italian tribes. But gradually it emancipated itself from the primitive tribal intergentilitial law. In keeping with the expansion of the Roman city-State into a world-empire, the *ius gentium* assumed the characteristic of an integrating world-law founded on the principle of the legal equality of all free human beings, as legal subjects in the inter-individual legal relationships. It was this private world-law which the classical Roman juris-consults connected with the Stoic conception of the *ius naturale*.

The Stoic idea of natural law in principle broke through the classical Greek idea of the city-State as the perfect natural community. It proclaimed the natural freedom and equality of all men as such. It is true that the Roman *ius gentium* did not entirely satisfy these principles of freedom and equality, insofar as it maintained slavery; nevertheless, it constituted an inter-individual legal sphere in which every free person was equally recognized as a legal subject independent of all specific communal bonds, even independent of Roman citizenship. This was the fundamental difference between the undifferentiated Quiritian tribal law and the private common law.

It was within this legal sphere that the undifferentiated authoritative proprietorial right, contained in the *dominium ex iure Quiritium*, was dissolved into a "*bonitary*" ownership lacking any authoritative character. Under the influence of the *ius gentium* the term *pater familias*, which in the ancient Quiritian tribal law meant the quality of domestic chief, was in its civil legal use transformed into a simple *nomen iuris* designating nothing but the abstract quality of a legal subject, belonging to every free person as such.

If we consider only the fact that the *ius gentium* even emancipated the function of legal subject from Roman citizenship, the question may arise as to whether this common law had anything to do with the structural principle of the State. One might suppose it was much more related to the Stoic idea of a temporal community of the whole of humankind. But we have seen in an earlier context that this universalist idea did not correspond to any structure of individuality in which a temporal community can only be realized.

To answer the question asked above, we should consider that the *ius gentium* could only become a real common private law by abstracting the legal relationships regulated by it from any specific non-juridical qualification. It may be that the Roman *societas*, as a contract of common law, took its origin in the Roman *familia*, later on oriented itself to occassional contractual cooperations for the purpose of economic profit or speculation, and finally to durable economically qualified undertakings. Nevertheless, its common law rules neither interfered with the internal sphere of the family, nor with that of industrial or commercial life. The same thing can be observed with respect to the other contracts regulated by the *ius gentium*, to the *jura in re* of the latter, to the common law rules concerning family law and hereditary right, *etc*.

### *The inner nature of the Roman ius gentium*

The common private law was only led by natural law principles of justice, the "nature of the matter," legal security, and equity, in their application to the inter-individual legal relationships of human beings as such. In this respect it was indeed the typical private legal correlate of the public communal law, which equally lacks a specific non-juridical qualification and is ruled by the principle of public interest. In addition, the *ius gentium* was a typical system of legal rules destined for the decision of law-suits by the common courts of the State. As to its formal juridical source it was praetorial law during the classical era of Roman jurisprudence. In its typical character as an integrating private common law it could not develop outside of the framework of the *res publica,* which was only able to *realize* the typical principles of the *ius gentium.* This realization was doubtless a matter of public interest, although the Roman lawyers emphatically established that, as to its inner nature, the common private law did not pertain to the *res publica* but to the interest of the individual legal subjects in their inter-individual relationships. The public interest was concerned with the private common law insofar as the *res publica,* by means of an impartial common jurisdiction, could prevent a complete disintegration of private law and a revival of the ancient undifferentiated legal spheres; for the latter were incompatible with the State's monopolistic organization of the sword-power and the public legal authority.

In this respect the sharp distinction between public and private law was a vital concern of the *res publica.* By controlling the jurisdiction over all private law-suits, in as much as they pertained to the sphere of common private law, the State was able to prohibit any attempt on the part of private power-formations to usurp an exclusive authority over the subjects of the body politic. Since the common private law was also sharply distinguished from all internal private legal spheres of a typical non-juridical qualification, its formation was by the nature of the case *bound to* the *res publica.* Outside of the latter there was not any room for an inter-individual common legal sphere based upon the natural law principle of equality of all free individuals as such. As to their inner nature the non-political societal relationships nowhere corresponded to this principle. But with respect to the State this principle was the natural correlate of the principle of the public legal equality of its subjects as to their common subjection to the public authority.

The distinction between *ius civile* and *ius gentium* was doomed to disappear, since under the influence of the praetorial law the former lost its material coherence with the archaic Roman tribal law and was almost completely accommodated to the *ius gentium.* In addition, Roman citizenship was to an ever increasing degree attributed to peregrines. In the classical period of Roman jurisprudence the victory of the *ius gentium* over the *ius civile* was already decided. JUSTINIAN's codification abolished the last remnants of the ancient civil law, which had long lost any practical significance.

It is true that, as to its material content, the formation of the private common law, at least in the classical period of Roman jurisprudence, was not due to the legislator but to the Roman lawyers. In this sense it was doubtless "*Juristenrecht.*" But the work of the juris consults was bound to the system of actions formed by the praetor. And it was by means of these actions that the State retained the legal control over the private common law-sphere, which apart from the *res publica* was doomed to disappear.

Legal history shows that this bond between the idea of a private common law, in the sense of the *ius gentium,* and that of the *res publica* is not an exclusive peculiarity of the Roman legal system. There is not any instance to be found of a private common law, in the sense defined above, which has developed outside of the State.

It may be that the Roman legal tradition has exercised a considerable influence upon the development of private common law in the modern continental States of Europe where the legislator has codified its rules. But in England the influence of Roman law was only small. Nevertheless here, too, a civil law-system has developed based on the essential principles of juridical equality and freedom of all individuals in their inter-personal civil legal relations. Here this development took place by means of a material transformation of the feudal law into a common private law. And it was brought about by the formative activity of judicial organs of the State, viz. the common law courts and the supplementary equity jurisdiction of the chancellor. The classical English jurists considered this common civil law as the expression of natural justice, just as the Roman lawyers had looked upon the *ius gentium* as the expression of the *ius naturalis.*

We could also point to the Scandinavian States whose common civil law has not undergone the influence of the Roman *ius gentium.*

### *The radical difference between common private law and the undifferentiated popular or tribal law*

Under the influence of the Historical School the erroneous conception arose that common civil law was nothing but the ancient folk or tribal law, developed in a technical sense by the jurists. This view was opposed to BODIN's idea of the sovereignty of the legislator with respect to the formation of civil law. The truth is that there is a radical difference in nature between primitive folk-law and the highly differentiated common private law; the latter could only develop after the material destruction of the undifferentiated primitive society of which the popular or tribal law was a juridical expression.

And this destruction was due to the rise of the State as a *res publica.*

Irrespective of the question as to whether the common private law has been codified by the legislator or has been preponderantly formed by the courts of the State, it is by its inner nature a legal sphere bound to the body politic. And the original competence to its formation cannot belong to any other organized community but the State. By means of this common private law the body politic can bind in an enkaptical way any specific (non-juridically qualified) private law to the principles of inter-individual justice, legal security and equity. But the internal spheres of these specific kinds of private law, qualified by the non-juridical leading function of the societal relationships to which they belong, remain exempt from the competence of the State. In the introduction to the general theory of the enkaptic structural interlacements we shall show that this thesis is not an arbitrary assumption due to a subjective political conviction. It will appear that it is rather founded in the structural conditions of every differentiated human society, which cannot be disregarded with impunity.

# Political Theories of the Modern Age[1]

The new humanistic ground-motive soon made its impact felt on the process of differentiation in society that had begun with the Renaissance. After the breakup of medieval ecclesiastical culture, the idea of the state began to break through in various countries in the form of absolute monarchies. Gradually absolute monarchs regained for the crown many of the prerogatives that had fallen into the hands of private lords under the feudal system. The new humanistic science ideal suggested an exact method by means of which this could best be done.

**State Absolutism**

Humanism did not acknowledge that governmental authority is limited intrinsically by societal spheres grounded in the creation order. Such a recognition contradicted the autonomy and freedom of human personality, which Humanism interpreted in accordance with its own religious ground-motive. As long as modern humankind expects freedom and independence from the advance of the new exact sciences, the motive of nature or control will also govern its view of society. The "modern age" demanded a "new construction." Humanistic thought directed itself particularly to the construction of the state. The new state, which was unknown in medieval society, was designed as an instrument of control that could gather all power to itself. Humanism assumed that science was as competent to construct this state as it was to manufacture the mechanical tools controlling the forces of nature. All current knowledge of society, which was still relatively incomplete, was consciously adapted to this constructionistic science ideal.

In sixteenth-century France Jean Bodin [1530-1596] laid the foundations for a humanistic political theory in his absolutistic concept of sovereignty. This concept formed the methodological starting-point and cornerstone for his entire political theory. For Bodin the essential characteristic of sovereignty lay in its absolute competence or power unlimited by positive juridical boundaries. Although in conscience the government might indeed be bound by natural and divine law, it nevertheless stands above all positive rules of law which derive their validity only from the will of the government itself. No law-giver [*rechtsvormer*] in the non-state spheres of life can appeal to a ground of authority that lies outside of the power of the state's sovereign legislator. In the whole of society the formation of law must depend solely on the will of the state's legislator, the only sovereign. Even customary law or common law,

---

[1] A section from Chapter Six of The Collected Works of Herman Dooyeweerd, Series B, Volume 3, [Roots of Western Culture], intitally published in English by Wedge Publishing Foundation, Toronto 1979, new edition with The Edwin Mellen Press (1999).

which in the Middle Ages was more significant than statutory law, was subject to either the implicit or explicit approval of the sovereign. The necessity of this requirement was understandable, since customary law clearly bore the stamp of an undifferentiated feudal system, the mortal enemy of the modern state.

The humanistic concept of sovereignty did not merely declare war on the undifferentiated societal relationships of the "Dark Ages." Inspired by the modern ideal of science, it also aimed at guiding the incipient process of differentiation in order to guarantee the absolute sovereignty of the state over all the remaining life spheres. Among the differentiated societal bonds, the church had been the state's most powerful rival. But now the time had arrived to bring the church under the sovereignty of the state. The Reformation and subsequent conflicts within Protestantism had excited denominational passions, and the unrest of the churches spilled over into politics, threatening the peace and unity of the state. Political Humanism had only one remedy for this; viz., intervention by the state in the internal affairs of the church in order to force the church into a position of "tolerance" which would bring peace and unity back into the body politic.

This was also the solution offered by Hugo Grotius, an adherent of Bodin's concept of sovereignty. Grotius was not only a representative of "biblical Humanism," but also the founder of the humanistic theory of natural law. This new doctrine of natural law was also one of the heralds of the modern age. It became the champion for the reconstruction of the legal system necessitated by the breakthrough of the modern idea of the state. It sought a point of contact with classical Roman law with its sharp distinction between public law and private civil law, and, like the Roman jurists, based the latter in a law of nature whose basic principles were the inherent freedom and equality of all human beings. This humanistic doctrine of natural law stood in clear opposition to the undifferentiated indigenous law of the Germanic nations which was viewed as being in conflict with "natural reason." Over against this, Grotius and his immediate followers intended to derive a comprehensive system of legal rules from the "rational, social nature" of humankind. Independently of human institutionalization, these rules were to hold for all times and all nations. To this end they employed the new mathematical and scientific method, the ground and certainty of modern humanity. In reality, however, it was largely classical Roman law that furnished the "rules of natural law." Grotius sought an autonomous basis for his doctrine of natural law, independent of ecclesiastical authority. As he himself declared, this foundation would hold even if God did not exist. As a "biblical humanist" he hastily added that denying the existence of God is reprehensible; but this admonition did not alter the fact that for him an appeal to the "natural, social nature" of a person was sufficient for the validity of natural law.

Grotius's standpoint was completely different from the position of Thomas Aquinas which was based on the Roman Catholic ground-motive of nature and grace. Thomas indeed taught that a person can know certain principles of natural law and natural morality by the natural light of reason independent of divine revelation. But in the final analysis Thomas always referred these principles back to the "rational" wisdom of God the creator. Thomas and the other scholastics would never think of searching for an autonomously valid ground of natural law in "natural human reason" alone, a ground independent of even the existence of God. Only in the heretical trends of late scholasticism, which completely separated nature and grace, did these tendencies appear. Grotius's conception of the basis of natural law as independent of the existence of God was a harbinger of the process of emancipation and secularization which came to fruition during the Enlightenment. The new humanistic freedom motive was the starting-point of this process.

Characteristic of the new doctrine of natural law was its individualistic construction of societal spheres, particularly the sphere of the state. As long as the motive of nature and control was dominant in the humanistic doctrine of natural law, theorists unanimously defended Bodin's absolutistic concept of sovereignty. Because its consistent application left no room for the free personality, the concept of sovereignty was made acceptable through the construction of a "social contract." It was argued that by means of a social compact the originally free and equal individuals had surrendered their natural freedom voluntarily in order to bind themselves as a body politic. This was generally followed by a contract of authority and subjection, in which the people conferred authority to a sovereign and pledged obedience. In this way the free and autonomous individual consented to the absolute sovereignty of a ruler. Such an individual could therefore never complain of injustice.

**Critical Turning Point**

When Humanism accented the natural-scientific motive of control rather than the motive of freedom, it sought the ultimate ground of certainty in mathematical and natural-scientific thinking. Humanists were convinced that only the method of thought developed by modern mathematics and natural science teaches human beings to know reality as it is "in itself," stripped of all the subjective additions and errors of human consciousness which victimize us in the naive experience of daily life. The new ideal of science came with great pretensions! It alone could unveil the true order and coherence of reality.

However, precisely at this point the first misgivings about the value of the exact sciences arose. The location of the ground of certainty lay in the exact concepts of subjective consciousness. But the more human beings explored this subjective consciousness itself, the more insistent the question of the actual *origin* of mathematical and natural-scientific concepts became. From where did these concepts derive their content? One could not deny that children and primitive peoples did not possess them. They must therefore have originated in the course of time. But from what did we form them? Here the problem of theoretical knowledge was immediately cast into *psychological* terms. It was assumed that inner human consciousness had only one window to the reality of the "external world." This window was sensory perception as it functioned in the aspect of feeling. If consistently carried through, this assumption implies that the origin of mathematical and natural-scientific concepts can only lie in the sense impressions of the external world. But from these impressions one could derive neither exact mathematical relationships nor the mechanical laws of cause and effect that constituted the foundation of classical mechanics. Perception merely taught that there is a temporal sequence of sense impressions from fact A to fact B. It never demonstrated that B always and necessarily follows A, and yet this demonstration was what the laws of physical science required.

Faced with this predicament, the conclusion was reached that we cannot know to what extent the exact natural sciences assist us in understanding *reality*. Why then, we may ask, do we still accept the laws of causality? At this point Humanism showed that it was unwilling to abandon its new science ideal. Its solution was as follows: if the law of cause and effect does not make us understand the coherence of reality as it is in itself, then this law must at least refer to a mechanical connection between our sense impressions.

David Hume's well-known theory of the association of impressions and representations was the model for this view. The Scottish thinker Hume [1711-1776] explained the sequence of cause and effect entirely in terms of psychical association, arguing that if we repeatedly observe fact B following fact A, then at our next perception of A we necessarily connect A with the representation of B.

The critique of scientific thought begun by John Locke and continued by David Hume struck a serious blow to the "metaphysical" pretensions of the deterministic science ideal which claimed that science could furnish knowledge of reality as it is "in itself," that is, independent of human consciousness. It seemed that the freedom motive, which had suffered under the overextension of the nature motive, might free itself from the deterministic ideal of science. If the natural-scientific laws do not correspond with objective reality, then science cannot claim the right to deny the freedom of one's thought and will. But were modern people prepared to pay this price for reinstating their awareness of freedom and autonomy? Would they sacrifice the foundations of their science ideal to this end?

The epistemological attack on the science ideal was only a prelude to a widespread and critical reversal within the humanistic attitude to life. After their initial intoxication with science, modern thinkers began to reflect on the deepest religious root and motive in their lives. This deepest root was not modern natural science but the humanistic religion of personality with its motive of freedom. If the deterministic science ideal was unable to give the autonomous freedom of a person its just due, then it should not occupy the dominant place in the humanistic world view. If this is the case, then it is erroneous to search for the essence of a person in scientific thought; and then it is imperative that the motive of control, the dynamic behind the science ideal, be deprived of its religious priority. Primacy belongs to the freedom motive instead.

It was Jean-Jacques Rousseau [1712-1778] who called Humanism to this critical self-examination. In 1750 he became famous overnight by submitting a paper in response to a competition organized by the university of Dijon. The topic was a favorite Enlightenment theme: what have modern science and culture contributed to the freedom and happiness of humanity? Rousseau's answer was a passionate attack both on the supremacy of science in life and on all of modern, rationalistic culture. Rousseau argued that science had exchanged freedom and equality for slavery. Also in his later writings Rousseau remained a spokesman for the humanistic freedom motive. For him the root of human personality lay not in exact scientific thought but in the feeling of freedom.

Rousseau's humanistic religion was not one of reason but of feeling. When he claimed that religion resides in the heart rather than in the mind, he regarded the "heart" not as the religious root of human life, as the scriptures teach, but as the seat of feeling. He also interpreted the nature motive in terms of a natural feeling of freedom. The original natural state of human beings was a condition of innocence and happiness; individuals lived in freedom and in equality. But rationalistic culture brought humankind into slavery and misery. It created inequality and subjected nations to the rule of kings. As a result, no trace was left of the free and autonomous human personality.

Nevertheless, Rousseau did not believe that a return to the happy state of nature was possible. He had no desire to abandon the modern idea of the state. Rather, he sought to conceive of a body politic that would conform fully to the freedom motive of modern humanity. He envisioned a state in which individuals, after relinquishing their natural freedom and equality, could regain them in a higher form.

Certainly, in the first phase of Humanism, Grotius, Hobbes, and other proponents of natural law attempted to justify the absolute sovereignty of the ruler before the forum of the humanistic freedom motive. Their point of departure too was a "state of nature" characterized by freedom and equality. The notion of a social contract was required to justify governmental authority. Under such a contract individuals voluntarily surrender their natural freedom and equality. In complete autonomy, they place themselves under a government. In this way, individuals can transfer their natural authority to the government, retaining nothing for themselves. *Volenti non fit iniuria*: no injustice is done to one who wills it. One cannot complain of injustice if one agreed to the institution of absolute government.

John Locke [1632-1704] was among the first modern thinkers not satisfied with this natural-law construction of an absolute state. His starting-points were the inalienable rights of life, property, and freedom, which could not be surrendered even in a contract. From the outset, therefore, Locke limited the content of the social contract to the goal of the peaceful enjoyment of one's natural human rights in a civil state. Individuals relinquished to the government only their natural competence to defend their rights on their own behalf against intrusion from others. In this way Locke laid the basis for the classical liberal view of the state. According to this liberal approach the state is a limited liability company organized to protect the civil rights of life, liberty, and property.

Thus already in Locke's classical liberal idea of the state we discover a reaction of the freedom motive against the nature motive which had governed the earlier conceptions of natural law. Rousseau, however, was not satisfied with this reaction. Like Locke, he proceeded from the free and inalienable rights of a person. But Rousseau went beyond the essentially private-legal human rights, which constitute the foundation of private civil law, to the public-legal guarantee of the freedom and autonomy of human personality in the inalienable rights of the citizen. In this way Rousseau is the founder of the classical humanistic idea of democracy which soon clashed with the classical liberal conception of the state.

### Classical Liberalism

"Freedom and equality!" This was the indivisible slogan of the French Revolution, the death warrant for the remnants of the old regime [*ançien régime*]. It was inscribed in blood. Both during and after the Restoration period many spoke of the hollow and unrealistic tone of these revolutionary concepts. Such criticisms, however, were mistaken, and as a result many arrows missed the mark in attempts made to refute the principles of the French Revolution.

Undoubtedly, the principles of the French Revolution were governed by the humanistic ground-motive. Locke and Rousseau were its apostles. However, the "natural-law" theories of these thinkers aimed at two concrete goals: a) the breakthrough of the *idea of the state* in terms of the final breakdown of the undifferentiated feudal structures; and b) the breakthrough of the fundamental idea of civil law, i.e., the *idea of human rights*. These goals could indeed be realized because they were entirely in line with the process of differentiation which had begun after the Middle Ages in western society and which was founded in the divine order for human history. Both goals presupposed the realization of freedom and equality in a specifically *juridical* sense, and not, for example, in an economic or social sense. Further, both belonged together; a civil-legal order cannot exist without the order of the state.

An authentic state is not really present as long as the authority to govern in effect belongs, *as a feudal right*, to the private prerogatives of a ruler who in turn can convey, sell, or lend them to officials of his realm or even to private persons. According to its nature and inner structure, the state is a *res publica*, a "public entity." It is an institution qualified by public law, a community of government and subjects founded typically on a monopoly of sword power within a given territory. As Groen van Prinsterer declared in his second period, every true state has a republican character.

Thus the division of the forms of the state into monarchies and republics commonly made since Machiavelli is basically incorrect. The word *republic* indicates nothing whatsoever about the form of government. It merely signifies that the state is a public rather than a private institution. But the word *monarchy* does pertain to a form of government; the government here is monarchical, that is, a single person is the head of government. Conversely, the word monarchy does not relate to the question of whether a monarchy complies with the character of the state as a republic. Throughout the course of history many monarchies have lacked the character of a state, since governmental authority functioned not as an office serving the *res publica* but as the private property of a particular ruler. Governmental jurisdiction was an undifferentiated feudal prerogative. In such cases one should speak not of a state but of a realm (*regnum*), which was the property of a king. Not every realm is a state.

Nevertheless, the monarchical form of government is not incompatible with the character of a republic. Royal authority can function as the highest office within the *res publica*. The opposition between "monarchy" and "republic" arose only because the undifferentiated view of royal authority, as a private prerogative of the ruler, was maintained for such a long time precisely in the monarchical setting. This is also the reason why so many natural-law theorists in the humanist tradition linked the idea of the state to the idea of popular sovereignty. It seemed that only the sovereignty of the people complied with the view that the state is a *res publica*. Furthermore, in the light of the religious ground-motive of Humanism, popular sovereignty seemed the only way to justify governmental authority before the forum of the free and autonomous human personality.

Thomas Hobbes, with his keen intellect, quickly detected the weakness in the conception of popular sovereignty in which the people and the state were identified. After all, in this construction the "people" was but an aggregate of *individuals* who contracted with each other to relinquish their freedom and equality and thus entered a state relationship. But Hobbes clearly saw that without a government this "people" cannot form a political unity, a *state*. Only in the person of the government does the people become a corporate body capable of acting on its own. The government *represents* the unity of the people. For this reason Hobbes rejected the notion that people and government can be viewed as two equal parties that enter into a contract to settle the content of governmental authority. In view of this, Hobbes had no use for the notion of popular sovereignty which supposedly existed prior to and apart from the body politic. Only the *government*, as representative of the unity of the people, is the true *sovereign*. The people could never protest against the sovereign's injustice, since its actions comprised the actions of the people. Although Hobbes first attempted to justify the absolute monarchy of the Stuarts, he had little difficulty in isolating his position from the monarchical form of government when the Puritan Revolution temporarily unseated the Stuarts, establishing authority of the English parliament. Sovereignty could also be vested in a body like parliament.

John Locke's classical liberal political theory was directed against Hobbes's absolutistic concept of sovereignty that left the people unprotected from their ruler. Locke reinstated popular sovereignty as the basis for the republican character of the state. However, he did not commit the error of linking popular sovereignty to a specific form of government, arguing only that the democratic form of government in the sense of a representative government guarantees the people's freedom best. For Locke the crown merely represented the sovereign people even in an autocratic, monarchical form of government. If it was clear that the king no longer promoted the cause of the people and the common good, and if the people lacked democratic and parliamentary institutions, then the people could resort to revolution. In such a case the people only exercise their original right of sovereignty, for a despotic monarch who merely pursues his private interests is not the head of state but just a private person.

Thus in Locke the idea of the representation of the people acquired a *republican* sense that was genuinely related to the idea of the *state*. This republican feature distinguished the modern idea of representation from the feudal practices of the Middle Ages, when the estates (nobility, clergy, and townsmen) acted as the representatives of their respective "subjects" before their lords.

Locke's political theory is a prime example of classical liberalism because he views the state as an association among individuals entered into for the purpose of establishing organized protection of the natural, inalienable human rights; i.e., liberty in the sense of private autonomy, property, and life. These natural human rights constitute the basis for the sphere of civil private law where all individuals without discrimination can enjoy legal freedom and equality. These rights were not transferred to the state in the social contract. The social compact transfers to the state only one's natural freedom to *defend* one's right to life, liberty, and property. In civil society every person is free, by means of labour, to acquire private property and to dispose of it autonomously. This freedom is guaranteed by the power of the state and subject to limitations required by the common good in accordance with the law.

The social contract is thus the avenue by means of which individuals decide to enter into the body politic for a specific and limited purpose. But the social contract also comprises a contract of authority whereby these individuals subject themselves once and for all to the will of the majority in the exercise of the most prominent right of sovereignty, viz., the institution of the power of legislation. The sovereign people thus possess what French theorists describe as the *pouvoir constituant*, the original legal power to institute a legislative body. The people exercise this legislative power only by means of *representation*, not *directly* as Rousseau argued in his radical democratic conception.

Locke's liberal conception of the state did not imply a universal right to vote on the part of every citizen. He was perfectly satisfied with a limitation of the franchise to a socially privileged class, as was the case in the English constitutional monarchy of his day. Freedom and equality in "civil society," in the private-legal order, did not at all imply equality in the political rights of the citizens, and certainly not a so-called "economic democracy." Locke's democratic ideal did not extend beyond the demands that the king exercise legislative power only through parliament, the constitutional representative of the people, and that the king be subject to all of parliament's laws. His democratic ideal directed itself only against the private prerogative and divine right [*droit divin*] of the monarch, since both contradicted the humanistic idea of freedom and autonomy of the human personality, oriented to what the English call "the rule of law." Locke's ideal must be understood against the background of the constitutional monarchy of William of Orange. Later this ideal itself came into conflict with the notion of radical democracy, the political gospel preached by Rousseau on the eve of the French Revolution.

For classical liberalism democracy was not an end in itself. Rather, it was a *means* to protect private civil rights. When democracy was later elevated to be an end in itself [*Selbstzweck*] on the basis of the humanistic freedom motive, democracy developed in an anti-liberal manner. This line of development was Rousseau's.

After Locke, the classical liberal idea of democracy was linked with the idea of the separation and balance of the legislative, executive, and judicial powers of the state. The French thinker Montesquieu [1689-1755] was a major advocate of this doctrine. Taken together, then, the following configuration of ideas comprises the classical liberal idea of the law state [*rechtsstaat*]:[1] the state is a representative democracy founded in popular sovereignty, subject to the constitutional supremacy of the legislature though with the greatest possible separation and balance of the state's three powers, and organized to protect the individual's civil rights. One can find a penetrating analysis of this position in the excellent dissertation by J.P.A. Mekkes, entitled *The Development of the Humanistic Theories of the Constitutional State*.[2]

The humanistic freedom motive distinctly inspired the liberal idea of democracy. But in the context of classical liberalism this motive was expressed only in the doctrine of *inalienable human rights*, in the principles of civil legal freedom and equality. As we noted above, the political equality of citizens was definitely not a part of liberalism. The doctrine of the *inalienable rights of citizens*, in the sense of Rousseau's radical democratic theory, is not of liberal origin.

But does this liberal conception of the constitutional state embody the principle of pure democracy as seen in accordance with the humanistic freedom motive? Not at all! The entire principle of representation, especially when it is severed from the notion of universal franchise, is inherently at odds with the principle of pure democracy. Unquestionably, the liberal idea presupposed an aristocratic and elite foundation. The legislature merely *represented* the people within the republic. With or without the cooperation of a monarch, it exercised legislative authority *independently* of its constituents. The legislature was a people's elite chosen according to the liberal standards of intellectual ability and wealth. The voters themselves belonged to an elite. According to liberal criteria, only they were capable of fulfilling this special political function. In view of his radically democratic standpoint, Rousseau's judgment of this highly esteemed English liberalism was surprisingly mild when he wrote: "the English people believe that they are free. But they are mistaken. They are free only while choosing members of Parliament."

---

1 The term *rechtsstaat* will as a rule be translated as "*constitutional state*" or "*constitutional state under the rule of law*."

2 J.P.A. Mekkes, *Proeve eener critische beschouwing van de ontwikkeling der humanistische rechtsstaatstheorieën* (Utrecht/Rotterdam: Libertas, 1940).

In reality, the impact of classical liberalism on the development of the modern constitutional state is a direct result of the absence of a consistent application of the democratic principle. This does not mean that liberalism with its individualistic, humanistic basis and application – is acceptable to us. But we appreciate its blend of monarchic, aristocratic, and democratic elements which Calvin already recommended as a basis for the relatively best form of the state. Moreover, the principle of the independence of parliament over against the electorate is fully in harmony with the state as *res publica*. Further, the principle of an elite – when divorced from its indefensible ties to land ownership, capital, or the intellect – is an aristocratic element which the modern literature on democracy increasingly recognizes as a necessary counter-force to the anarchistic influence of the "masses" in government policy. Finally, Montesquieu's famous teaching on separation and balance of powers within the state contains an important kernel of political wisdom which is easily overlooked by those critics who only see the untenability of this theory.

Certainly, little effort was needed to demonstrate the impossibility of an absolute separation of the legislature, the executive, and the judiciary powers in the persons who occupied these offices. Opponents quickly pointed out that the separation of powers was not found in the English constitution, as Montesquieu had claimed. In our day some have attempted to salvage Montesquieu's theory on the separation of powers by interpreting it as a mere separation of constitutional functions which could be combined in the same office-bearer. But this "correction" cuts the heart out of Montesquieu's theory by interpreting it in a purely *legal* sense while it was intended as a *political* guideline. The French thinker aimed at a balance of *political* powers within the structure of the state. He sought to achieve this balance by placing the "aristo-democratic" power of the people in the legislature and the "aristo-cratic" or monarchic power in the actual administration of the country's affairs. It was clear that in his conception, juridical power as such could have no *political* significance. For this reason he referred to this power as a kind of "nullity" [*en quelque façon nulle*] and as the mere "mouthpiece of the law" [*la bouche de la loi*]. From a constitutional point of view this of course cannot be maintained. The power of the judiciary, itself devoid of political significance, should not however be subject to the political influence of either the legislature or the executive. It had to function in the "balance" of powers for the protection of the rights of the individuals.

Viewed in this light, we see that Montesquieu merely elaborated the principle of "moderation" [*modération*] in democracy by a balanced blend of monarchical and aristocratic political forms. This was entirely in keeping with the liberal framework of Locke's representative democracy. Locke too considered a balance of political powers essential, which was quite in harmony with the *juridical* supremacy of the legislator. He attempted to achieve this balance by limiting the frequency and duration of the legislative sessions, so that the executive branch in fulfilling its task would not be unduly influenced by political pressure from parliament. Although he did not include the judiciary in his triad of powers, Locke explicitly maintained that the independence and impartiality of the courts are necessary conditions for guaranteeing the liberties and rights of the individual.

What also deserves our attention is that the parliamentarism which developed in England under the foreign House of Hanover did not agree with the classical liberal idea of democracy. The political hegemony given to parliament and, behind it, to the political party electorally victorious under its "leader," was clearly in conflict with the liberal idea of balancing political powers. Parliamentarism in England was curbed by the nation's self-discipline, adherence to tradition, sportsmanlike spirit of "fair play," respect for individual rights, and acceptance of the principle of elitism. But in a country like France parliamentarism was easily transformed into a full-fledged radical democracy. The executive was reduced to a political tool of the assembly, and in turn the assembly became a political tool of the masses.

**Radical Democracy**

Modern commentators on democracy are fond of contrasting liberalism and democracy. Liberalism, they argue, is based on the principle of freedom; democracy, by contrast, on the principle of equality. When they battled their common foe – namely, the remnants of feudalism – the contrast between these two basic principles was not yet clear. As a result, the French Revolution was waged under the slogan of freedom, equality, and brotherhood.

But this approach is certainly based on a misunderstanding. It is an error caused by a lack of insight into the classical humanistic meaning of the concepts of freedom and equality. To be sure, a fundamental contrast exists between liberalism and radical democracy. Liberalism advocates a moderate democracy tempered by representative institutions, a balance between the monarchical power of the ruler and the legislative power of the assembly or parliament, and the independence of the judiciary to guarantee the individual citizen's private rights of freedom.

Radical democracy could accept neither the representative system nor the liberal idea of separating and balancing political powers. Nevertheless, as long as radical democracy rested on its classical humanistic basis, it too was driven, in an even more fundamental way, by the humanistic motive of freedom. Rousseau, the apostle of radical democracy, was also the spokesman for the humanistic ideal of freedom. He was the first thinker to attach religious primacy to the humanistic freedom motive, above the humanistic nature motive. To him autonomy, the free self-determination of human personality, was the highest religious good which far surpassed the classical science ideal of controlling natural phenomena through the natural-scientific research methods of the mind. In Rousseau's radically democratic idea of the state, equality of citizens constituted a radical application of the humanistic principle of freedom in the structuration of the state.

For Locke, the father of classical liberalism, democracy was not an end in itself. It was merely a means to protect the private autonomy of the individual in the free disposition of his property rights. Equality in his view belongs to the private-legal sphere of civil law – the sphere of *civil society*. The conception of natural law during his day was primarily concerned with retaining as much *natural* freedom as possible, the freedom that one enjoyed before the state was instituted. Locke made no radical attempt to apply the humanistic freedom motive to the exercise of political rights. He never referred to inalienable *constitutional* rights of citizens or to *constitutional* equality of citizens. For him it was self-evident that an elite composed of the educated and of the rich should be the active participants in legislation. Even the election of legislators was limited to an elite. A large majority of citizens was expected to be content with a passive role in politics.

But for Rousseau the crucial issue was *political* freedom. He concerned himself with the inalienable rights of the citizen [*droits du citoyen*], in which the rights of human beings [*droits de l'homme*] were to be given *public-legal* expression. Rousseau was as it were religiously obsessed with guaranteeing the autonomous freedom of human personality within the constraints of the state. No element of free self-determination could be lost when individuals made the transition from the state of nature to the state of citizenship. If one surrendered but a part of one's natural freedom in the social contract without receiving it again in the higher form of the inalienable rights of active citizenship, then self-determination was unattainable. To Rousseau a representative system like England's assaulted the free self-determination of humankind. Sovereign people cannot be "represented," for representation forces the people to surrender their rights of free self-determination to an elite which can then impose its own will on the people again and thus enslave them.

The liberal idea of separating political powers was entirely unacceptable to Rousseau for the same reason. The sovereignty of the people is indivisible, since the people's inalienable right of free and sovereign self-determination is itself indivisible. What does it profit people – in Rousseau's humanistic frame of reference – if they retain part of their private, natural freedom over against the state, but then subject themselves to laws not of their own free making in their *public* position as citizens? A state of this kind is clearly illegitimate over against the inalienable claims of human personality. It remains an institution of slavery. Only in a state based on unfreedom and domination – a state therefore which is *illegal* before the tribunal of the humanistic ideal of personality – does the need arise to protect the private rights of individuals, the need to keep intact the remnant of natural liberties over against the tyrant.

But a state which is an authentic expression of the humanistic idea of freedom cannot possibly recognize the *private* freedom of the individual *over against* itself. Such a state must completely absorb the natural freedom of a person into the higher form of political freedom, of active citizenship rights which inherently belong to all citizens equally and not merely to an elite among them. In a truly free state the individual cannot possess rights and liberties over against the *res publica* because in such a state the total freedom of the individual must come to expression.

In Rousseau's natural-law conception of radical democracy, the individuals surrender all their natural freedom to the body politic in order to receive this freedom back, in a higher political sense, as members of the state. In a free state every citizen without distinction becomes a part of the sovereign people, a body which sets the law for itself. The right of legislation cannot be transferred; it is the primary right of the sovereign people itself. The law must be the expression of the truly autonomous communal will, the *volonté général*, which is never oriented to a private interest but always serves the public interest [*salut public*]. A true law cannot grant privileges to particular persons or groups, as in the feudal system. If the law imposes public burdens, they must affect all citizens *equally*. Here too the freedom of the body politic requires that all citizens be equal before the law. The government of the land can possess neither political power nor legal authority of its own. As magistrates, the rulers are merely servants of the sovereign people, removed at will.

Like Hobbes's Leviathan, Rousseau's radical democracy is totalitarian in every respect. It expresses the humanistic motive of freedom in a radically political way, in absolute antithesis to the biblical creation motive underlying the principle of sphere sovereignty. The notion of radical democracy contains the paradoxical conclusion that the highest freedom of a person lies in the utter absolutism of the state. As Rousseau declared: "a person must be forced to be free" [*On les forcera d'être libre*].

But this criticism may not blind us to the important elements of truth in Rousseau's classical humanistic conception of democracy. In distinction from the undifferentiated feudal notions of governmental authority, Rousseau's idea of the state pointedly brought the *res-publica* conception to the foreground. He still viewed equality, the foundation of democracy, in a strictly political sense as an outgrowth of the citizen's freedom within the state. Rousseau was not a victim of the inner decay of the democratic idea that we see around us today when people rob the principle of equality of its typically political meaning by applying it indiscriminately to all relationships of life. Surely, some of these leveling tendencies were noticeable among certain revolutionary groups during the French Revolution. Communism had already begun to announce its presence. But these trends could not persevere as long as the classical idea of the state, though itself a humanistic absolutization, retained its hard-won hold on the minds of people. The battle between "freedom" and "equality" could begin only when the idea of the state itself was drawn into Humanism's most recent process of decay.

# Glossary

[The following glossary of Dooyeweerd's technical terms and neologisms is reproduced and edited by Daniël F. M. Strauss, with the permission of its author, Albert M. Wolters, from C. T. McIntire, ed., *The Legacy of Herman Dooyeweerd: Reflections on Critical Philosophy in the Christian Tradition* (Lanham MD, 1985), pp. 167-171.]

THIS GLOSSARY OF HERMAN DOOYEWEERD'S terms is an adapted version of the one published in L. Kalsbeek, *Contours of a Christian Philosophy* (Toronto: Wedge, 1975). It does not provide exhaustive technical definitions but gives hints and pointers for a better understanding. Entries marked with an asterisk are those terms which are used by Dooyeweerd in a way which is unusual in English-speaking philosophical contexts and are, therefore, a potential source of misunderstanding. Words or phrases in small caps and beginning with a capital letter refer to other entries in this glossary.

* **Analogy** (see LAW-SPHERE): Collective name for a RETROCIPATION or an ANTICIPATION.
* **Anticipation**: An ANALOGY within one MODALITY referring to a later modality. An example is "efficiency," a meaning-moment which is found within the historical modality, but which points forward to the later economic modality. Contrast with RETROCIPATION.
* **Antinomy**: Literally "conflict of laws" (from Greek *anti*, "against," and *nomos*, "law"). A logical contradiction arising out of a failure to distinguish the different kinds of law valid in different MODALITIES. Since ontic laws do not conflict (Principium Exclusae Antinomiae), an antinomy is always a logical sign of ontological reductionism.
* **Antithesis**: Used by Dooyeweerd (following Abraham Kuyper) in a specifically religious sense to refer to the fundamental spiritual opposition between the kingdom of God and the kingdom of darkness. See Galatians 5:17. Since this is an opposition between regimes, not realms, it runs through every department of human life and culture, including philosophy and the academic enterprise as a whole, and through the heart of every believer as he or she struggles to live a life of undivided allegiance to God.
* **Aspect**: A synonym for MODALITY.
* **Cosmonomic idea**: Dooyeweerd's own English rendering of the Dutch term *wetsidee*. Occasionally equivalents are "transcendental ground idea" or "transcendental basic idea". The intention of this new term is to bring to expression that there exists an unbreakable coherence between God's *law* (nomos) and created reality (*cosmos*) factually subjected to God's law.

**Dialectic**: In Dooyeweerd's usage: an unresolvable tension, within a system or line of thought, between two logically irreconcilable polar positions. Such a dialectical tension is characteristic of each of the three non-Christian GROUND-MOTIVES which Dooyeweerd sees as having dominated Western thought.

*****Enkapsis (enkaptic)**: A neologism borrowed by Dooyeweerd from the Swiss biologist Heidenhain, and derived from the Greek *enkaptein*, "to swallow up." The term refers to the structural interlacements which can exist between things, plants, animals, and societal structures which have their own internal structural principle and independent qualifying function. As such, enkapsis is to be clearly distinguished from the part-whole relation, in which there is a common internal structure and qualifying function.

**Factual Side**: General designation of whatever is *subjected* to the LAW-SIDE of creation (see SUBJECT-SIDE).

**Founding function**: The earliest of the two modalities which characterize certain types of structural wholes. The other is called the GUIDING FUNCTION. For example, the founding function of the family is the biotic modality.

***** **Gegenstand**: A German word for "object," used by Dooyeweerd as a technical term for a modality when abstracted from the coherence of time and opposed to the analytical function in the theoretical attitude of thought, thereby establishing the Gegenstand relation. Gegenstand is therefore the technically precise word for the object of SCIENCE, while "object" itself is reserved for the objects of NAIVE EXPERIENCE.

**Ground-motive**: The Dutch term *grondmotief*, used by Dooyeweerd in the sense of fundamental motivation, driving force. He distinguished four basic ground-motives in the history of Western civilization:

(1) form and matter, which dominated pagan Greek philosophy; (2) nature and grace, which underlay medieval Christian synthesis thought (3) nature and freedom, which has shaped the philosophies of modern times; and (4) creation, fall, and redemption, which lies at the root of a radical and integrally scriptural philosophy.

**Guiding function**: The highest subject function of a structural whole (e.g. stone, animal, business enterprise, or state). Except in the case of humans, this function is also said to QUALIFY the structural whole. It is called the guiding function because it "guides" or "leads" its earlier functions. For example, the guiding function of a plant is the biotic. The physical function of a plant (as studied, e.g. by biochemistry) is different from physical functioning elsewhere because of its being "guided" by the biotic. Also called "leading function".

***** **Heart**: The concentration point of human existence; the supratemporal focus of all human temporal functions; the religious root unity of humans. Dooyeweerd says that it was his rediscovery of the biblical idea of the heart as the central religious depth dimension of human multifaceted life which enabled him to wrestle free from neo-Kantianism and phenomenology. The Scriptures speak of this focal point also as "soul," "spirit," and "inner man." Philiosophical equivalents are Ego, I, I-ness, and Selfhood. It is the heart in this sense which survives death, and it is by the religious redirection of the heart in regeneration that all human temporal functions are renewed.

* **Immanence Philosophy**: A name for all non-Christian philosophy, which tries to find the ground and integration of reality *within* the created order. Unlike Christianity, which acknowledges a transcendent Creator above all things, immanence philosophy of necessity absolutizes some feature or aspect of creation itself.

* **Individuality-structure**: This term represents arguably one of the most difficult concepts in Dooyeweerd's philosophy. Coined in both Dutch and English by Dooyeweerd himself it has led sometimes to serious misunderstandings amongst scholars. Over the years there have been various attempts to come up with an alternate term, some of which are described below, but in the absence of a consensus it was decided to leave the term the way it is.

It is the general name or the characteristic law (order) of concrete things, as given by virtue of creation. Individuality-structures belong to the law-side of reality. Dooyeweerd uses the term individuality-structure to indicate the applicability of a structural order *for* the existence of *individual* entities. Thus the *structural laws* for the state, for marriage, for works of art, for mosquitoes, for sodium chloride, and so forth are called individuality-structures. The idea of an individual whole is determined by an individuality-structure which precedes the theoretical analysis of its modal functions. The identity of an individual whole is a relative unity in a multiplicity of functions. (See MODALITY.) Van Riessen prefers to call this law for entities an *identity-structure*, since as such it guarantees the persistent **identity** of all **entities** (*Wijsbegeerte*, Kampen 1970, p.158). In his work (*Alive, An Enquiry into the Origin and Meaning of Life*, 1984, Ross House Books, Vallecito, California), M. Verbrugge introduces his own distinct systematic account concerning the nature of (what he calls) *functors*, a word first introduced by Hendrik Hart for the dimension of individuality-structures (cf. Hart: *Understanding Our World, Towards an Integral Ontology*, New York 1984, cf.pp.445-446). As a substitute for the notion of an individuality-structure, Verbrugge advances the term: *idionomy* (cf. *Alive*, pp.42, 81ff., 91ff.). Of course this term may also cause misunderstanding if it is taken to mean that each individual creature (subject) has its *own unique* law. What is intended is that every *type of law* (*nomos*) is meant to delimit and determine unique subjects. In other words, however *specified* the universality of the law may be, it can never, in its bearing upon unique individual creatures, itself become something *uniquely individual*. Another way of grasping the meaning of Dooyeweerd's notion of an *individuality-structure* is, in following an oral suggestion by Roy

Clouser (Zeist, August 1986), to call it a *type-law* (from Greek: *typonomy*). This simply means that all entities of a certain *type* conform to this law. The following perspective given by M.D. Stafleu elucidates this terminology in a *systematic way* (*Time and Again, A Systematic Analysis of the Foundations of Physics*, Wedge Publishing Foundation, Toronto 1980, p.6, 11): *typical laws* (type-laws/typonomies, such as the Coulomb law – applicable only to charged entities and the Pauli principle – applicable only to fermions) are special laws which apply to a limited class of entities only, whereas *modal laws* hold universally for all possible entities. D.F.M. Strauss ('*Inleiding tot die Kosmologie*', SACUM, Bloemfontein 1980) introduces the expression *entity structures*. The term **entity** comprises both the *individuality* and the *identity* of the thing concerned – therefore it accounts for the respective emphases found in Dooyeweerd's notion of *individuality-structures* and in Van Riessen's notion of *identity structures*. The following words of Dooyeweerd show that both the **individuality** and **identity** of an entity is determined by its 'individuality-structure': "In general we can establish that the factual temporal duration of a thing as an individual and identical whole is dependent on the preservation of its structure of individuality" (*A New Critique of Theoretical Thought*, Vol.III:79).

**Irreducibility (irreducible)**: Incapability of theoretical reduction. This is the negative way of referring to the unique distinctiveness of things and aspects which we find everywhere in creation and which theoretical thought must respect. Insofar as everything has its own peculiar created nature and character, it cannot be understood in terms of categories foreign to itself.

* **Law**: The notion of creational law is central to Dooyeweerd's philosophy. Everything in creation is subject to God's law for it, and accordingly law is the boundary between God and creation. Scriptural synonyms for law are "ordinance," "decree," "commandment," "word," and so on. Dooyeweerd stresses that law is not in opposition to but the condition for true freedom. See also NORM and LAW-SIDE.

**Law-Side**: The created cosmos, for Dooyeweerd, has two correlative "sides": a law-side and a factual side (initially called: SUBJECT-SIDE). The former is simply the coherence of God's laws or ordinances for creation; the latter is the totality of created reality which is subject to those laws. It is important to note that the law-side always holds universally.

**Law-Sphere** (see MODAL STRUCTURE and MODALITY): The circle of laws qualified by a unique, irreducible and indefinable meaning-nucleus is known as a law-sphere. Within every law-sphere temporal reality has a modal function and in this function is subjected (French: *sujet*) to the laws of the modal spheres. Therefore every law-sphere has a law-side and a subject-side that are given only in unbreakable correlation with each other. (See DIAGRAM on p.127.)

* **Meaning**: Dooyeweerd uses the word "meaning" in an unusual sense. By it he means the referential, non-self-sufficient character of created reality in that it points beyond itself to God as Origin. Dooyeweerd stresses that reality *is* meaning in this sense and that, therefore, it does not *have* meaning. "Meaning" is the Christian alternative to the metaphysical substance of immanence philosphy. "Meaning" becomes almost a synonym for "reality." Note the many compounds formed from it: meaning-nucleus, meaning-side, meaning-moment, meaning-fullness.
* **Meaning-nucleus**: The indefinable core meaning of a MODALITY.
**Modality** (See MODAL STRUCTURE and LAW-SPHERE): One of the fifteen fundamental ways of being distinguished by Dooyeweerd. As modes of being, they are sharply distinguished from the concrete things which function within them. Initially Dooyeweerd distinguished fourteen aspects only, but since 1950 he introduced the kinematical aspect of *uniform movement* between the spatial and the physical aspects. Modalities are also known as "modal functions," "modal aspects," or as "facets" of created reality. (See DIAGRAM on p.127.)
**Modal Structure** (see MODALITY and LAW-SPHERE): The peculiar constellation, in any given modality, of its meaning-moments (anticipatory, retrocipatory, nuclear). Contrast INDIVIDUALITY-STRUCTURE.
* **Naive experience**: Human experience insofar as it is not "theoretical" in Dooyeweerd's precise sense."Naive" does not mean unsophisticated. Sometimes called "ordinary" or "everyday" experience. Dooyeweerd takes pains to emphasize that theory is embedded in this everyday experience and must not violate it.
**Norm (normative)**: Postpsychical laws, that is, modal laws for the analytical through pistical law-spheres (see LAW-SPHERE and DIAGRAM on p.127). These laws are norms because they need to be positivized (see POSITIVIZE) and can be violated, in distinction from the "natural laws" of the pre-analytical spheres which are obeyed involuntarily (e.g., in a digestive process).
* **Nuclear-moment**: A synonym for MEANING-NUCLEUS and LAW-SPHERE, used to designate the indefinable core meaning of a MODALITY or aspect of created reality.
* **Object**: Something qualified by an object function and thus correlated to a subject function. A work of art, for instance, is qualified by its correlation to the human subjective function of aesthetic appreciation. Similarly, the elements of a sacrament are pistical objects.
**Opening process**: The process by which latent modal anticipations are "opened" or actualized. The modal meaning is then said to be "deepened." It is this process which makes possible the cultural development (differentiation) of society from a primitive ("closed," undifferentiated) stage. For example, by the opening or disclosure of the ethical anticipation in the juridical aspect, the modal meaning of the legal aspect is deepened and society can move from the principle of "an eye for an eye"

to the consideration of extenuating circumstances in the administration of justice.

* **Philosophy**: In Dooyeweerd's precise systematic terminology, philosophy is the encyclopedic science, that is, its proper task is the theoretical investigation of the overall systematic integration of the various scientific disciplines and their fields of inquiry. Dooyeweerd also uses the term in a more inclusive sense, especially when he points out that all philosophy is rooted in a pretheoretical religious commitment and that some philosophical conception, in turn, lies at the root of all scientific scholarship.

**Positivize**: A word coined to translate the Dutch word *positiveren*, which means to make positive in the sense of being actually valid in a given time or place. For example, positive law is the legislation which is in force in a given country at a particular time; it is contrasted with the *legal principles* which lawmakers must positivize as legislation. In a general sense, it refers to the responsible implementation of all normative principles in human life as embodied, for example, in state legislation, economic policy, ethical guidelines, and so on.

**Qualify**: The GUIDING FUNCTION of a thing is said to qualify it in the sense of characterizing it. In this sense a plant is said to be qualified by the biotic and a state by the juridical [aspects].

* **Radical**: Dooyeweerd frequently uses this term with an implicit reference to the Greek meaning of *radix* = *root*. This usage must not be confused with the political connotation of the term *radical* in English. In other works Dooyeweerd sometimes paraphrases his use of the term radical with the phrase: *penetrating to the root of created reality*.

* **Religion (religious)**: For Dooyeweerd, religion is not an area or sphere of life but the all-encompassing and direction-giving root of it. It is service of God (or a substitute no-god) in every domain of human endeavor. As such, it is to be sharply distinguished from religious faith, which is but one of the many acts and attitudes of human existence. Religion is an affair of the HEART and so directs all human functions. Dooyeweerd says religion is "the innate impulse of the human selfhood to direct itself toward the *true* or toward a *pretended* absolute Origin of all temporal diversity of meaning" (*A New Critique of Theoretical Thought*, Vol.I, 1953, p.57).

* **Retrocipation**: A feature in one MODALITY which refers to, is reminiscent of, an earlier one, yet retaining the modal qualification of the aspect in which it is found. The "extension" of a concept, for example, is a kind of logical space: it is a strictly logical affair, and yet it harks back to the spatial modality in its original sense. See ANTICIPATION.

* **Science**: Two things are noted about Dooyeweerd's use of the term "science". In the first place, as a translation of the Dutch word *wetenschap* (analogous to the German word Wissenschaft), it embraces all scholarly study – not only the natural sciences but also the social sciences and the humanities, including theology and philosophy. In the second place, sci-

ence is always, strictly speaking, a matter of modal abstraction, that is, of analytically lifting an aspect out of the temporal coherence in which it is found and examining it in the Gegenstand relation. But in this investigation it does not focus its theoretical attention upon the modal structure of such an aspect itself; rather, it focuses on the coherence of the actual phenomena which function within that structure. Modal abstraction as such must be distinguished from NAIVE EXPERIENCE. In the first sense, therefore, "science" has a wider application in Dooyeweerd than is usual in English-speaking countries, but in the second sense it has a more restricted, technical meaning.

**Sphere Sovereignty**: A translation of Kuyper's phrase *souvereiniteit in eigen kring*, by which he meant that the various distinct spheres of human authority (such as family, church, school, and business enterprise) each have their own responsibility and decision-making power which may not be usurped by those in authority in another sphere, for example, the state. Dooyeweerd retains this usage but also extends it to mean the IRREDUCIBILITY of the modal aspects. This is the ontical principle on which the societal principle is based since each of the societal "spheres" mentioned is qualified by a different irreducible modality.

* **Subject**: Used in two senses by Dooyeweerd: (1) "subject" as distinguished from LAW, (2) "subject" as distinguished from OBJECT. The latter sense is roughly equivalent to common usage; the former is unusual and ambiguous. Since all things are "subject" to LAW, objects are also subjects in the first sense. Dooyeweerd's matured conception, however, does not show this ambiguity. By distinguishing between the *law-side* and the *factual side* of creation, both subject and object (sense (2)) are part of the factual side.

**Subject-Side**: The correlate of LAW-SIDE, preferably called the factual side. Another feature of the factual subject-side is that it is only here that individuality is found.

**Substratum**: The aggregate of modalities *preceding* a given aspect in the modal order. The arithmetic, spatial, kinematic, and physical, for example, together form the substratum for the biotic. They are also the necessary foundation upon which the biotic rests, and without which it cannot exist. See SUPERSTRATUM (and the DIAGRAM on p.127).

**Superstratum**: The aggregate of modalities *following* a given aspect in the modal order. For example, the pistical, ethical, juridical and aesthetic together constitute the superstratum of the economic. See SUBSTRATUM.

* **Synthesis**: The combination, in a single philosophical conception, of characteristic themes from both pagan philosophy and biblical religion. It is this feature of the Christian intellectual tradition, present since patristic times, with which Dooyeweerd wants to make a radical break. Epistemologically seen the term *synthesis* is used to designate the way in which a multiplicity of features is integrated within the unity of a concept. The re-union of the logical aspect of the theoretical act of thought

## POLITICAL PHILOSOPHY

with its non-logical 'Gegenstand' is called an inter-modal meaning-synthesis.

* **Time**: In Dooyeweerd, a general ontological principle of intermodal continuity, with far wider application than our common notion of time, which is equated by him with the physical manifestation of this general cosmic time. It is, therefore, not coordinate with space. All created things, except the human HEART, are in time. At the law-side time expresses itself as time-order and at the factual side (including subject-subject and subject-object relations) as time duration.

**Transcendental**: A technical term from the philosophy of Kant denoting the *a priori* structural conditions which make human experience (specifically human knowledge and theoretical thought) possible. As such it is to be sharply distinguished from the term "transcendent." Furthermore, the basic (transcendental) Idea of a philosophy pre-supposes the transcendent and central sphere of consciousness (the human HEART). This constitutes the *second* meaning in which Dooyeweerd uses the term transcendental: through its transcendental ground-Idea philosophy points beyond itself to its ultimate religious foundation transcending the realm of thought.

# CREATURES SUBJECTED TO CREATIONAL LAWS

## Aspects, Entities and Societal Institutions

| Law-Spheres (Aspects) | Meaning-nuclei |
|---|---|
| Certitudinal ▲ | certainty (to be sure) |
| Ethical ▲ | love/troth |
| Juridical ▲ | retribution |
| Aesthetical | beautiful harmony |
| Economical ▲ | frugality/avoid excesses |
| Social | social intercourse |
| Sign-mode | symbolical signification |
| Cultural-historical ▼ | formative power/control |
| Logical | analysis |
| Sensitive-psychical | sensitivity/feeling |
| Biotical | organic life |
| Physical | energy-operation |
| Kinematic | unif. motion/constancy |
| Spatial | continuous extension |
| Numerical | discrete quantity |

HUMAN BEINGS — SOCIAL LIFEFORMS & CULTURAL THINGS

Family, State, Church, Business

ANIMALS / PLANTS / THINGS

▼ Foundational function of church, state and business
▲ Qualifying function

# Index

## A
Alciat 54
Althusius 2, 26, 56-57
analogical moments 66
anthropology 5
Arendt 8
Augustine 3, 10, 12, 38-39

## B
Bahr 78-79
Barth 14, 24, 53
Belgic Confession 32, 41
Below 85-86
Beseler 59
Beugnot 58
Bodin 2, 53-58, 60-61, 86, 94-96
body politic 69, 72-87, 89-90, 92-93, 95-96, 98, 100-101, 105-106
brotherhoods 47
Brunner 14, 24

## C
Calvin 1-2, 15, 20, 24-26, 29-31, 39, 54, 56
Calvinism 1, 15, 29
Carney 2
Chesterton 6
Chlodovech 90
Christian state 14-16, 20-21, 24, 30, 41-42
Christianity 1, 15-16, 19, 35, 43-44
church-fathers 38
church-institute 19-21, 23, 26, 29, 32, 37, 41, 48, 66
Civil
 – Code 46, 51
 – law 46-51, 58, 60-61, 67-68, 77-78, 88, 90, 92-93, 95, 99, 104
 – rights 98, 102
 – society 101, 104
classical liberal idea of the state 99
Common
 – good 8, 39-40, 42, 101
 – grace 3, 16, 33, 39, 42
concept of sovereignty 52-55, 57-66, 68, 94-96, 100
constitutional state 58, 60, 62, 102
creation ordinances 4

## D
differentiated responsibility 4
differentiated societal collectivities 47
divine world-order 25-26, 31, 56-57, 75
dominium ex iure Quiritium 91
Dooyeweerd 2, 5-13
Doumergue 29
Duez 89
Duguit 50, 63

## E
Easton 7
ecclesiastical creed 41
Eigeman 29
Ellul 7-8
Elshtain 8
empirical reality 11
Engels 7
enkaptic structural interlacements 93
Enlightenment 46, 48, 97

## F
Fascism 14, 18, 40, 42
feudal system 47, 85-86, 94-95, 106
Fichte 76, 87
Final Treaty of Vienna 58
folk-law 59-62, 93
foundational function 39, 70-73, 75-76, 78, 81, 83
founding function 11-12, 37-38
Francis I 54
fraternities 47
Free University 3, 5
French Revolution 2, 29, 73, 99, 102, 104, 106
Friedman 6

## G

gentilitial political power 69
Gerber 60-61
Gierke 82
Gneist 78-79
Grant 1, 7-8
Greco-Roman political theory 26
Greek philosophy 17
Groen van Prinsterer 2, 99
Grotius 87
Gurvitch 63-64

## H

Hamel 71
Historical School of Law 45
Hobbes 2, 4-5, 10, 27-28, 45, 57-58, 98, 100, 106
Holy Roman Empire 54
Hugo Grotius 28-29, 57, 95
humanistic philosophy 15, 27, 56
Humboldt 76
Hume 97

## I

Idsinga 85
immanence-philosophy 76
individualism 3, 28, 46
individuality-structure 35-37, 70, 72-75, 83, 85, 89
ius
   – civile 47, 92
   – commune 49, 67, 90
   – gentium 45-48, 50, 90-93
   – naturale 47-50, 57, 60, 90
   – specificum 67-68

## J

Jellinek 60-61, 63
justice 6, 8-13, 19, 28, 32-35, 39, 41-42, 49, 71, 73, 76, 78, 88-89, 91, 93, 96, 98, 100

## K

Kalsbeek 11
Kant 76-78, 87-88
Kelsen 79-81, 85
kingdom of God 14, 16-17, 19-21, 25, 31, 42

Krabbe 63
Kuyper 1-5, 9, 12, 15, 31-33

## L

Laband 60-61
laissez faire 28
Lasswell 7
law of gravity 36
law-gospel polarity 23
law-spheres 32-36, 41
Lex
   – duodecim tabularum 90
   – Salica 90
Locke 6-7, 28, 58, 97-105
Louis XVIII 58
Luther 21, 23-24, 31

## M

Machiavelli 99
Melanchthon 23, 26
Middle Ages 14, 17, 22, 24, 56, 85-86, 94, 99, 101
monarchical republic 69
Montesquieu 58, 102-103
Morgenthau 9-11
motive of freedom 56, 96-97, 104, 106
Mott 10-11
Mussolini 74

## N

National-Socialism 14, 18, 40, 42
natural law 12, 28-29, 40, 45-48, 53, 56-61, 63, 76, 86-87, 90-92, 95-96, 98-99, 104
nature and freedom 56, 62
nature and grace 21-23, 95
nature-grace scheme 24
Niebuhr 3, 10-11
nomen iuris 91
nominalism 22-23, 25, 27

## O

organized communities 45, 64, 70, 81
organized power 7, 72-74
Otto Gierke 29, 59

## P

pater familias 42, 47, 91
personality-ideal 27

Plato 7, 10, 12-13
polis 12, 38, 50, 67, 70, 72-74, 81, 92
political
- authority 10-11, 69
- philosophy 2, 56, 76
- realism 10-12
- science 7, 52-53, 64
- theory 1-2, 6, 11, 13, 23-24, 26, 38-39, 57, 86-87, 94, 100-101
pouvoir constituant 101
Preusz 52, 62
private law 42, 46-51, 77, 82, 85-86, 90-93, 101
Protestantism 95
public
- interest 55, 69, 84, 87-91, 106
- law 40, 42, 46, 50, 61, 67-68, 77, 79-80, 82, 84-85, 87-88, 90, 95, 99
- legal community 50, 82, 84
Pufendorff 87

## Q

qualifying function 11, 35-39, 49, 51, 67, 70, 76, 81

## R

radical democracy 102, 104-106
ratio scripta 46-47, 50
Reformation 1-2, 14, 21, 23, 26, 53, 68, 95
regnum 86, 100
religious neutrality 5
res
- in commercio 55
- publica 55, 60, 69, 81, 84, 86, 91-93, 99-100, 105
- regia 69
Restoration 58, 99
Roman
- Catholic Church 14
- law 42, 46, 55, 60, 62, 92-93, 95
- societas 91
Roth 86
Rousseau 2, 12, 28, 57-58, 87, 97-99, 101-102, 104-106
royal rights 47

## S

Sabine 1
salus publica 50-51, 87-89
Schelling 59
science-ideal 27, 45
separating political powers 105
Skinner 1
social rank 48
societal
- differentiation 9
- structures 16, 19-20, 29-30, 32, 38, 72, 75-76, 83, 86-87
sociological doctrine of law 45-46
Sohm 86
source of law 60, 62
sovereignty of law 63-64
Soviet Republics 51
Sphere sovereignty 3
sphere-universality 34-35
Stahl 78-79
state sovereignty 2
state-absolutism 28-29, 64
statutory law 94
Strauss 8

## T

Tawney 1
the modern state 95
Themis 50
third Empire 71, 80
Thomas Aquinas 5, 12, 17, 20, 22, 25, 38, 95
Thomasius 29
Thomism 22
totality-idea 20
transcendental Idea 75
typical leading function 12, 76, 81

## U

undifferentiated
- communities 9
- organized community 70
universalistic theory 83

## V

variability-types 72
Voegelin 8
Volenti non fit iniuria 98

voluntarism 22
von Hayek 6
von Jhering 46-47
von Savigny 59-60

# W

Waite 86
Weber 1
Western culture 26
William of Occam 22

William of Orange 102
Wolff 76, 87-88
Wolin 8
Wolters 1
Wolterstorff 1
world-order 17, 19, 25-26, 28-29, 31, 34, 56-57, 75

# Z

Zasius 54

www.ingramcontent.com/pod-product-compliance
Lightning Source LLC
Chambersburg PA
CBHW032042290426
44110CB00012B/912